CW00848037

Cumbrian Language
in its Cultural Context

Simon Roper

Til Anne & David

First Printing 2020

ISBN 9798662603677

Foreword

I write this book in a bit of a hurry so as to put to paper some ideas I have had about the development of the Cumbrian dialect of English. I have always borne a particular interest in Cumbrian, because although my immediate family do not speak it in any meaningful way most of the time, it has left its mark very clearly on the speech of the older members of my family, who were involved in upland farming in their youth.

Being an interest that arose from what I felt was an emotional connection to my heritage, it started out (when I was maybe fifteen or sixteen) with a huge amount of confirmation bias; I loved the idea that the culture of my great-grandparents was unique. I grabbed at any potential Scandinavian loan-word I could find, assuming, for example, that a word like *attercop* (spider) must have come from Old Norse, because I noticed that the Norwegian *edderkopp* (spider) sounded similar. However, I did not consider that an Old English cognate might provide an even closer match - *āttercoppe*.

My examination of the dialect was largely without knowledge of phonological processes, and was highly unscientific - but my interest in language began to branch out into Old English and Old Norse, and to modern languages such as German (which I can communicate in, as long as the listener isn't too picky about grammar). The idea that sounds could correspond between languages, as they do between English accents, appealed to me, and so I started to see if the same concept could be applied to Cumbrian. I realised that a lot of my earlier considerations had been wrong, and that I needed to properly study phonology if anything useful was to come of the interest.

Since I began taking an active interest in phonological change, a lot of things began falling into place, and that is how this book has come about. I do not know how long it will be, and that's not necessarily the point - I am not overly concerned how many people read it. Nonetheless, I will try to make it reasonably accessible to a reader who does not know about linguistics, so that they can avoid making the same mistakes I did when I started, and perhaps investigate further on their own.

The changes I describe here will in many cases have been described before (for instance in the enormously useful *Researching Northern English,* edited by Raymond Hickey), but in some cases I am not aware of them having been written about elsewhere. Many of the changes I describe may also have occurred in neighbouring dialects, and may therefore have been described in literature I have not come across.

It is also important to note that I am not a linguist: at the time of writing I have only just finished a BSc dissertation in Archaeology, although my being on an integrated Masters course means I have not actually got the degree yet. I am an enthusiast, and I would encourage and appreciate that anybody who finds errors in this to let me know.

I hope this book is enjoyed by all who read it, whether you are a linguist or a layman.

Note on Orthography

With no standard system of spelling to default to, writers in the Cumbrian dialect have gone about spelling Cumbrian words in a number of ways. Some have kept fairly rigidly to the southern English standard, either in that they have not reflected dialectal pronunciations in spelling at all, or they have used the same spelling as a similar-sounding standard English word where possible (in the *Glossarium Brigantinum*, the word /lɛːk/ 'to play' is given as *lake*). Some have used a divergent system of spelling, including spelling words in the *stone* and *book* lexical sets using innovative digraphs like *eá* and *eú*.

Others have made liberal use of apostrophes to indicate where sounds usually present in standard English are seen as having been elided. It might be argued that this is a dismissive technique, framing the dialect as a reduced or simplified standard English rather than a valid language variety in its own right, but I don't see any reason to presume malicious intent on the part of the writers who did it.

In example sentences, I have tried to imitate 19th-century authors, although I have sometimes used the digraphs <ya> and <iu> for words in the *stone, book* sets. In the glossaries, I have preferentially used spellings found in the relevant literature.

Note on Variety

Cumbrian may be viewed as a segment of a northern English (and southern Scottish) dialect contimuum, rather than a homogenous isolate. As a result, there is great linguistic variety within Cumbria, and this text will not be able to cover every version of Cumbrian that has existed within the last thousand years. Unique varieties of the dialect will have been 'concreted over' by subsequent influence from the mainstream variety. Because it is the most easily reconstructable, this book will focus on that mainstream variety - the progression that goes most directly from Northumbrian Old English to later Cumbrian. Anybody who is interested in 'dead end' varieties of the dialect - those whose uniqueness was largely lost due to mainstream influence - may find something interesting in the fourth selected text towards the end of this book. It is advised that readers who want a full picture of this author's views on the development of the dialect read at least until the end of the chapter on the possible Scottish origins of the long vowels.

Future Work

This book, while hopefully reasonably thorough, mostly covers the period between 1300 and 2000 in relatively light detail. There is some discussion of pre-1300 processes, but this is very underdeveloped. I hope, at some point, to write something that tracks north-western English from the Old English period to the Modern English period in as much detail as can be drawn out of the relevant texts. Until then, this will have to do.

Contents

An Introduction to Linguistics

Because a lot of this book will use quite technical language in order to clearly lay out what I am trying to say, here is an introduction to the linguistic principles that will be mentioned, for the layman. The linguistic portion of this book may well be difficult to understand without reading this section, and it may help to use some online resources as well, although hopefully that will not be necessary.

First, it's important to recognise that writing and speaking are two very different things. Letters are not the same things as sounds. This is exemplified by the fact that different languages may use the same letters to spell what are, in reality, different sounds. Even if you've never learnt a foreign language, you'll probably know that the letter 'r' represents a different sound for an English-speaker than it does for a French-speaker: most English speakers pronounce it with the tongue approaching the little ridge just above the teeth, but not quite touching it, and often involves the lips being nearly closed. A French speaker pronounces it as a gutteral sound at the back of the throat. Your exact pronunciation of the sound will vary depending on where you were brought up.

Unfortunately, this disconnect between letters and sounds means that we cannot necessarily look at a historical text and know exactly how it's meant to be pronounced; for all we know, the letters the author uses may have represented different sounds to themselves than they do to a modern reader. Linguists must employ more complicated methods in order to work out how older forms of English were pronounced, a bit like a detective reconstructing a crime scene. This is what I will attempt to do with Cumbrian in the first part of this book, although as you will see, a lot of the work has already been done for me by linguists writing in the 19th and 20th centuries. I will describe some of these forensic methods in this section, but if you're familiar with them, you can skip it.

Having acknowledged the disconnect between letters and sounds, how can linguists write what they're talking about in a succinct way? You could just write 'the English *r* sound' or 'the French *r* sound,' but even this is imprecise; the sounds will be different from place to place, and they may change over the course of the coming centuries, rendering it a useless description for future linguists.

We overcome this problem using an alphabet called the IPA (International Phonetic Alphabet). This alphabet can be used to represent pronunciation objectively; there is a different way of writing every single sound that the human vocal tract can produce, and it's used in the same way no matter what your first language is. IPA transcriptions are written either in /slashes/, or in [square brackets]. I'll explain why later in this chapter.

The *r* sound used in most English accents is written using the symbol /ɹ/, and the French sound is /ʁ/. You can use the IPA to show the differences between regional accents, as well. Take the word *butter*; in southern England, it may be pronounced [ˈbʌtə]. In a general American accent, it may be [ˈbʌɾɚ].

Let's briefly analyse the difference between the two;

$$[\text{ˈbʌtə}] \qquad [\text{ˈbʌɾɚ}]$$

Ignoring the square brackets for the moment, both transcriptions have a little mark at the start, a bit like an apostrophe. This tells us that the following syllable is the stressed one; the one you put the emphasis on when you're talking. It's at the start of the word, which tells us the first syllable is stressed. Both accents have the same *b* sound and the same short *u* sound, as you can see.

However, southern British accents use what we call a plosive /t/ sound in the middle of the word. Americans tend to use what's called an alveolar tap, where the tip of the tongue 'taps' the ridge just above the teeth, making it sound more like a 'd'. Listen to a recording of an American speaking; when they say *butter,* it may sound like they're saying *budder*. You can see this difference recorded in the IPA transcriptions above.

The final difference is that southern British accents (apart from west country accents) are usually **non-rhotic.** This means that you do not actually pronounce the letter *r* unless it comes before a vowel. In the word *butter*, it does not come before a vowel, so it's not pronounced; instead, most British English speakers just use a central vowel, the same 'uh' sound as you would use at the start of the word *about*. American English speakers usually use this same vowel, but with the tongue shaped a bit as if they were going to say *r*, and with the lips closed a bit as well. This is called an **r-coloured vowel.**

Even this is not universal; speakers from New York or Boston may pronounce *butter* non-rhotically, with no *r* sound. Speakers from Devon, Ireland, Scotland or parts of Lancashire may pronounce it rhotically, with an *r* sound.

Linguists also use terminology and charts to describe how you pronounce a particular sound. Consonant sounds can be described in a variety of ways. Here are some of the key ones:

Plosive sounds involve storing up air in the mouth and then releasing it in a burst, like /p/, /b/ or /g/.

Fricative sounds involve holding the tongue somewhere and letting air pass through it. The sound is caused by the resulting friction. /s/, /z/, /f/.

Nasal sounds involve releasing air through the nose, for example /n/ or /m/.

Voiced sounds are made while 'buzzing' the voice box. You can tell if a sound is voiced by putting your fingertips against your Adam's apple (or where your Adam's apple would be), and seeing if you can feel a gentle buzzing. /v/, /z/, /d/ and /g/ are examples of voiced sounds.

Voiceless sounds are made without this buzzing, for example /f/, /t/ and /k/. You can identify them using the same method as you identify voiced sounds, but there will be no gentle buzzing.

A sound can have more than one of these characteristics, but not if those characteristics are opposite. For example, a sound can't be both **plosive** and **fricative** at the same time, but it can be both **plosive** and **voiced** (for example /b/, /d/ and /g/). It can also be **plosive** and **voiceless** (/p/, /t/ and /k/).

Consonants are also described in terms of where they come from within the vocal tract. For example, they may be:

Bilabial - Pronounced using both of the lips., like /b/.

Dento-labial - Pronounced using one lip and one row of teeth, like /v/ (which uses the bottom lip and upper teeth).

Interdental - Pronounced with the tongue between the teeth.

Dental - Pronounced with the tongue against the teeth.

Alveolar - Pronounced with the tongue against the ridge just above the gumline, like /t/ in most accents.

Palatal - Pronounced at the hard palate, the top of the mouth, for example /j/ (the *y* sound in *yes*).

Velar - Pronounced at the back of the roof of the mouth, like /g/.

Uvular - Pronounced at the back of the mouth, near the throat.

You could describe a sound as a **voiced velar plosive**; this would be /g/. The corresponding **voiceless velar plosive** would be /k/. Likewise, a **voiceless dento-labial fricative** would be /f/, and the corresponding **voiced dento-labial fricative** would be /v/. As you can see, by just changing one characteristic of a sound, you can turn it into a different sound entirely. Bear in mind that consonants actually exist on a spectrum - pronouncing sounds on a different part of the palate, or with the tongue poised in a different way, can change their quality, and so the terminology I have given here is not always precise enough. English only uses a handful of the sounds it's possible for a human to pronounce. Each language has its own **inventory** of sounds, and there will usually be some overlap between two languages' inventories; for example, both English and German have /b/, /d/ and /g/ sounds, but German doesn't have the English /w/ sound, and most dialects of English don't have the German /x/ sound (a voiceless velar fricative). If you don't have a particular sound in your language or accent, it can be hard to learn to pronounce that sound, but with some practice you can usually pick it up.

Vowels operate a bit differently. Linguists use a chart to show where and how vowels are articulated within the mouth;

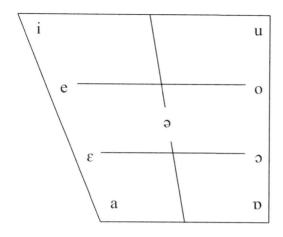

The above chart is only an outline with a few of the vowels marked; the IPA contains many more characters for vowels situated in various places on the chart. The position of a vowel on the chart indicates the position of the tongue in the mouth when one says the vowel; an **open** vowel is one articulated with the tongue low in the mouth, leaving the airway open (for example, /a/ or /ɒ/). These are sometimes called **low** vowels. A **close** vowel is the opposite; the tongue is high up in the mouth, partially closing off the airway (such as /i/ or /u/). These are sometimes called **high** vowels. A **front** vowel is articulated towards the front of the mouth, near the teeth and lips (like /i/ or /a/); a **back** vowel is articulated towards the back (like /u/ or /ɒ/). A vowel's position can be marked anywhere on the table.

We call this the vowel's **quality**, but vowels also differ in terms of **roundedness**. If a vowel is **rounded**, that means that you round your lips when you say it. An **unrounded** vowel is pronounced without the lips rounded. For example, /i/ is an unrounded vowel and /o/ is a rounded one. You can have pairs of vowels that share the same quality (i.e. are articulated in the same place in the mouth), but one is rounded and the other is unrounded.

Vowels can also differ in **length**; this is the length of time for which you are saying the vowel. In most dialects of English, the vowels in the first syllable of *father* and *water* are long; the vowels in *rot* and *up* are short. Some languages, like Spanish, do not make any distinction between long and short vowels at all. Most English dialects have two meaningful vowel lengths; short and long. Some languages have more than two vowel lengths, but these will not be relevant in this book.

The vowels I have described so far have been **monophthongs**. This means that while you're saying them, your tongue and lips remain in the same place, so you get a consistent vowel quality throughout. However, some vowel sounds are **diphthongs**, which means that something about their pronunciation changes while you're saying the vowel, so that they move from one quality to another. It's hard to come up with examples here, because some accents have diphthongs where others have monophthongs; many Scottish and northern English speakers have the vowel in *stone* as a monophthong, where many southern English and American speakers have it as a diphthong. The same is true of the word *name*. Try to pay attention to what your tongue and lips are doing while you say the vowel slowly; if they move over the course of you saying it, it's probably a diphthong. If they stay in the same place, it's likely to be a monophthong.

So now hopefully you have a basic grasp of the differences between sounds and how linguists talk about them. Next, we come to a rather more complicated idea; the idea of **phones** and **phonemes**. There is a subtle but very important difference between the two.

A **phone** is a specific, objective speech sound. It has specific acoustic properties, and is pronounced in a specific way. No matter your culture, no matter your language, a phone is a phone. If you look at a recording of a phone on a spectrogram, you can theoretically identify which phone it is.

A **phoneme** is a speech sound within the context of a particular language. In other words, it is what a speaker of a particular language or dialect considers to be a single speech sound. In actual fact, it may be pronounced in a number of different ways.

A phoneme can contain several phones, but a native speaker does not usually perceive the difference between them.

This is a tricky concept to grasp, so I'll give an example from English. Say the word *till,* and then say the word *still.* Focus very hard on how you pronounce the /t/ sound in these words. If you're a native English speaker, the chances are the /t/ in *till* sounds a little bit different than the /t/ in *still.* The /t/ in *still* may sound a little bit more like a 'd' sound. There is an acoustic difference between the two sounds; they're pronounced in two slightly different ways. The /t/ in *till* is aspirated, which means it's produced with a little burst of air, and the /t/ in *still* is unaspirated, which means it doesn't have as noticeable a burst of air. These are two separate **phones**, but as English speakers, we consider them to be basically the same sound, so in English they are **allophones** of the same **phoneme**.

The IPA can record things in two different ways; it can record words as clusters of phonemes, or as clusters of phones. If you're recording a word phonemically, you will normally do it in slashes, but if you're recording it phonetically, it is done with square brackets. To use the example of *till* and *still*, first giving phonetic transcriptions:

$$[t^hɪɫ] \quad [stɪɫ]$$

And then giving phonemic transcriptions:

$$/tɪl/ \quad /stɪl/$$

You'll notice that the phonetic transcription is much more specific, marking the aspiration difference between the /t/ sounds in the two words, which the phonological transcription does not mark. It also marks that the /l/ sound, at least in my accent, is pronounced further back in the mouth when it occurs at the end of a syllable; it is **velarised**. Both these ways of transcribing words are useful in their own way.

The underlying **phonological structure** of words is pretty stable from accent to accent, changing relatively little from place to place within the English language. Most of the differences in accent can be put down to differences in **phonetic realisation** - that is, differences in what phones are used for the various phonemes.

But why do we have different accents and dialects in the first place? Why do we have different languages? This is down to individual accents and dialects changing over time. If two groups of people start off speaking exactly the same, and the two groups don't communicate very much, their speech will slowly start to diverge, with one group developing a different accent from the other. These subtle changes in pronunciation will gradually drive the two ways of speaking to evolve into separate dialects, and given enough time, separate languages.

This means that it's sometimes hard to know whether two different ways of speaking are separate dialects or separate languages. Many consider broad Scots to be a different language to English. Many consider Austrian German to be a different language to the standard spoken in Germany. Speakers of Danish, Swedish and Norwegian can often understand each other without too much difficulty, just because their languages are so similar to one another; does this mean they are really all just dialects of one single language?

Linguists have not settled on any formal distinction, and many would argue that it doesn't really matter; it's just a semantic point, humans categorising things that don't really fall into neat categories. In my view, it is more relevant to politics than to the study of linguistics. Two groups may wish to be distinct, and so may categorise their ways of speaking as two different languages, even though they're quite similar. Opinions may differ within a community; some broad-speaking Scots may consider themselves to speak a dialect of English, some may consider themselves to speak a separate language.

In any case - why and how do languages change at all? There are enough factors contributing to this that numerous books have been written on the subject, and I can only provide a light summary here. The most relevant changes in this book are **sound changes**; instances of one speech sound turning into another. These can take a number of forms, and can happen for a number of reasons. There are several important things to bear in mind. Firstly, sounds are more likely to change to other sounds that are near to them in terms of articulation. For example, a /p/ can quickly change into a /f/, because these sounds both involve the lips. A /k/ can quickly turn into the sound /x/ (as found in the Scottish *loch*), because they are both articulated at the velum. A /k/ can turn into the affricate sound /t͡ʃ/, because although they are not articulated in the same place, /ʃ/ is articulated at the palate, which is close to the velum.

Secondly, sound change may be **conditioned** or **unconditioned**. A conditioned sound change happens only when the sound is in a certain environment. For instance, a /k/ sound may change into a /g/ sound, but only when it's at the end of a word. A /z/ could change to a /r/, but only between two vowels. An unconditioned sound change has no such conditions; the sound changes no matter what surrounds it.

A sound will change wherever its conditions are met - or, in the case of an unconditioned sound change, it will change wherever it appears in any word. You do not generally get sound changes that only affect one or two words. If you find something that resembles this, on closer inspection, there is normally another explanation for it. For example, one dialect with a sound change may have taken **loan words** from a nearby dialect without that sound change, making it look like those words avoided the sound change entirely.

Conditioned sound changes can sometimes cause sounds to split apart. For example, take the made-up words *tad* and *kal*. Let's transcribe these in IPA:

[tad]   [kał]

Let's say that, in this made-up language, you have a conditioned sound change where /a/ raises to /e/, but only before a plosive sound. In this case, it would change in *tad* (because /a/ is followed by /d/), but not in *kal* (because /a/ is followed by /l/, which isn't plosive). The result would be:

[ted]   [kał]

In this instance, the two vowel sounds have split apart, with one being affected by this conditioned change and the other being left behind because it did not meet the condition.

Likewise, sounds can sometimes merge together, becoming the same sound. For example, the words *what* and *when* used to have a voiceless sound at the beginning, sort of like a whispered /w/. Most readers will be familiar with it; the wispy *hwat* still present in the speech of some southern US and Scottish speakers. In most dialects, this has merged with the voiced /w/ sound in *water*. As a result, most English speakers use the same sound at the start of *what* as they do at the start of *water*. Such mergers can sometimes result in words becoming the same, for example *whales* and *wales*. To show this in IPA:

[ʍɛɪłz]   [wɛɪłz]

And after the merger:

[wɛɪłz]   [wɛɪłz]

Note that the IPA symbol /ʍ/ represents the voiceless version of /w/, and is not to be confused with /m/.

Now, an important principle here is that when two sounds have merged, they cannot un-merge along the same lines. Sound change has no memory; it can't remember which words were originally *wh-* words and which words were originally *w-* words. As people, we can tell because it's still shown in spelling, but as we've discussed, writing is not the same as speech. Mergers like this do not un-happen. An unrelated split may happen, but it's staggeringly unlikely to divide the words in exactly the same way as they were originally divided before a merger.

This is very useful to historical linguists, because it means that if two sounds are separate in a particular dialect, it means that those sounds cannot have merged in the past. This is obviously more complicated than it first appears; there are numerous situations where this rule can seemingly be flouted, but it's usually possible to spot these situations using clues. I will provide more information on this as and when it's needed over the course of the book[1].

Finally, sound change doesn't take grammar into account. Conditions for sound changes are usually not grammatical. For example, you would be unlikely to find a condition like '/e/ changes to /a/ but only in nouns.' Sound changes are mainly rooted in, and driven by, the phonology of a language, and the grammar is a separate thing from the phonology. There are circumstances in which sound change can actually cause grammatical change. To give an example, if grammatical cases and genders are only marked by verb endings, and those verb endings are subject to sound changes that weaken and level them so that they are indistinguishable from each other, then grammatical case and gender become meaningless in the language. This can be the result of something as simple as the weakening and centralising of vowels in short syllables.

Tangentially related to sound change, there are certain patterns

---

[1] This kind of thing could occur through cross-dialectal influence, although it would have to be quite drastic influence: if, for example, a dialect with merged *wh-* and *w-* existed next to a much more dominant dialect with the two sounds unmerged, the more dominant dialect could assert its influence such that the less dominant dialect might un-merge the two sets. The exact *nature* of this influence would be hard to describe in a footnote, and since this particular scenario hasn't actually played out in any English dialect I'm aware of, there doesn't seem much point. Such situations are surely rare, and will usually be discernable through clues.

that govern how sound inventories in languages work. Sound inventories are very likely to display a lot of **symmetry**. To give an example of a symmetrical vowel inventory, look at that of standard Castilian Spanish:

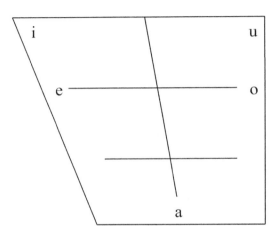

This system is symmetrical in that it has two front vowels, two back vowels and a central vowel. The two front vowels and the two back vowels are symmetrical in terms of openness (or **height**): /i/ is the same height as /u/, and /e/ is the same height as /o/. The system may be viewed in this way:

```
    i              u
    e              o
          a
```

While there are exceptions, there is a definite tendency towards symmetrical vowel inventories in modern languages, and this presumably applied to old languages as well. If a vowel inventory is asymmetrical, there is an increased likelihood that changes will happen to make it more symmetrical. For example, let's say that Spanish /i/ and /e/ were to merge, both becoming /i/, leaving the vowel inventory looking like this:

This vowel inventory now experiences pressure to become symmetrical again, for example by merging /o/ and /u/, or by having /i/ split back into /i/ and /e/ (although any such split would have to happen according to a condition that was valid in light of the original merger; as I've mentioned, sound change has no memory, so the merger could not happen in reverse).

There is some pressure on vowel inventories to avoid mergers where possible, because mergers can increase **ambiguity** in a language. If two very commonly-used vowels merge together, it's likely that several words (originally only separated by that one vowel difference) will become identical, and this will cause more confusion when people are speaking to one another.

As a thought exercise, you could imagine a hypothetical situation in which all of the vowels in English merged together and became /a/, in every word they occurred in. You can easily see how this change would cause massive confusion. Lots of words would end up sounding identical. *Ten, tin, ton* and *tan* would all be pronounced /tan/. *Meet, mate, moat* and *might* would all be /mat/.

So many words would become indistinguishable, in fact, that it would actually be more difficult to communicate ideas without confusion. Many sentences would have the potential to be misinterpreted. We naturally, unconsciously, tend to avoid this **ambiguity** by not allowing too many sounds to merge with one another. A certain amount of ambiguity is permissible in a language. For example, the words *meat* and *meet* used to be pronounced differently, but their vowels merged. They are used in such different situations from each other that it does not really matter that they sound identical.

In ordinary everyday speech, we do not get the words *meat* and *meet* mixed up with one another, because there are very few sentences affected. If I said 'I'm going to meet John,' you'd know exactly what I meant; you wouldn't be confused as to whether I meant *meet* ('encounter') or *meat* ('food')[2], because one is a verb, the other is a noun, and they mean entirely different things.

This means that vowels may exert certain pressures on each other in order for the wider vowel inventory to become symmetrical if it is not already. If a vowel's place of articulation moves, it is likely to have **pushing** and **pulling** effects on the vowels around it. All of these processes happen without people being aware of them; they are processes we are mostly unconscious of, but they are necessary to maintain a balance somewhere between ambiguity and impracticality. Everybody in a speech community is involved in regulating this, although they do not usually realise it. If two vowels drift to the point that they are very similar to each other, people within the speech community will generally still be able to differentiate between them, but they are unlikely to drift into a total merger if such a merger would impede a native speaker's ability to understand their own language.

This can sometimes result in significant changes that affect many vowels. One example of this is the **great vowel shift**, which occurred in southern England between the years 1400 and 1650. This affected all of the long vowels, and was an example of what we call a **chain shift**.

In a chain shift, sounds shift en masse; as one moves out of its position, another one is dragged in to replace it. All of the

---

[2] In writing, of course, we do not get them mixed up because they're spelled differently, but most spoken dialects of English have them pronounced identically. In fact, this difference in spelling exists because the words used to be pronounced with different vowel sounds. These vowels were merged in most English dialects by the late 1600s.

Middle English long vowels **raised**: in other words, people started to pronounce them with the tongue higher in the mouth. In the vowel chart we're now familiar with, they all moved upwards. Around 1400, they were in roughly these positions:

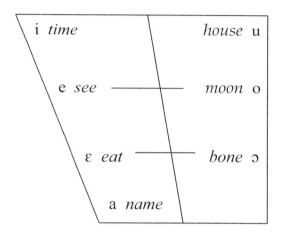

All of the vowels then raised in articulation, each one dragging the next one into its place; /ɔ/ became /o/, /o/ became /u/, /a/ became /ɛ/, /ɛ/ became /e/ and /e/ became /i/. You can see that in Middle English, the vowels in *time* /tiːm/ and *house* /huːs/ were about as raised as they could get. If they'd stayed put, /e/ would have raised and merged with /i/ and /o/ would have raised and merged with /u/. This would have introduced a lot of new ambiguity to the language. On the other hand, if both /i/ and /u/ had centralised, they would have run the risk of merging with each other, also increasing ambiguity.

What actually happened is that they underwent a process called **breaking**, or **diphthongisation**. This means that they turned from monophthongs to diphthongs. Judging by their development later on in the history of English, and also judging by the way these vowel qualities often diphthongise, they probably started off by gaining a more **central onset**, becoming [ɪi] and [ʊu] respectively. They would go further as time went on, but to keep it simple for the time being, the vowel qualities immediately post-vowel-shift were these:

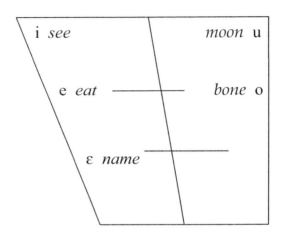

Since the great vowel shift, a number of further changes have happened in southern British English accents, so the above vowels are not representative of their qualities in any modern English accent I am aware of, although some of them persist in some varieties. While certain details of the great vowel shift are debated, this overview will hopefully be sufficient to explain the concept of chain shifts to the reader.

Sound changes, as well as gradual changes in meaning and grammar, steadily build over time, causing dialects and eventually languages to diverge from one another. As a result of this, you can find a lot of structural similarities between languages that might not be obvious upon first glance. For example, there is a lot of correspondence between sounds in

English words and sounds in German words with roughly the same meanings.

Note that I say 'correspondences,' and do necessarily mean 'similarities'; the German /aɪ/ diphthong is not that similar to the RP English /əʊ/ diphthong, but they correspond with each other very, very regularly: *stone* and *Stein*, *bone* and *Bein*, *home* and *Heim*, *token* and *Zeichen* ('sign'). The sounds do not correspond in all cases, but it is widespread enough to indicate a relationship, particularly as it occurs in such common, everyday words.

A useful concept here, and throughout this book, is that of **lexical sets**. A lexical set is a group of words that share a particular characteristic. For instance, you could have a lexical set of words that included the short vowel /a/, like *cat, rattle, sack* and *attack*. You could have a lexical set of words that included the consonant /ʃ/, like *shake*, *ash*, *mesh* and *sheep*. Lexical sets do not always totally overlap from dialect to dialect, let alone from language to language. For example, some American varieties of English have *dot, daughter* and *father* in the same lexical set, all having the vowel /ɑ/. Most British accents have them in three separate sets.

The last thing I want to establish in this chapter, just because it will be occasionally referred to, is the relationship between English and other European languages. These relationships form a sort of family tree, although this is a simplistic way of looking at it; the reality is often a lot fuzzier. A diagram of them can be found overleaf.

The diagram shows that English, German, Dutch and a number of other languages are descended from Proto-Germanic, a language spoken in Scandinavia around two thousand years ago. Despite how it may sound, Proto-Germanic was very different from modern German in terms of both its phonology and its grammar. Even though the language is not written down anywhere, it is possible to reconstruct a lot of Proto-Germanic vocabulary using our understanding of the rules of sound change, the pronunciation of modern Germanic languages and the written literary traditions we have from earlier Germanic

languages, such as Old English, Old Norse and Old High German.
Proto-Germanic will occasionally be mentioned throughout this book, but a deep understanding of it is not necessary.

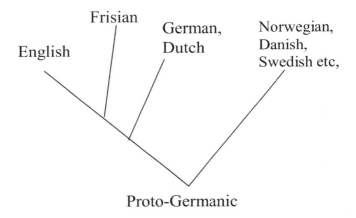

Late Cumbrian Phonology.

In recent years (relative to the time of writing), much uniquely Cumbrian vocabulary has become archaic, understood only by older people, or in many cases, by nobody at all. The phonology has been greatly diluted, as the phonology of many other northern English dialects have, as a result of the widespread ease of communication that has come about since the 1940s. However, we have older speakers (whose pronunciation surely preserves older forms), and several useful pieces of literature, particularly the *Grammar of the Dialect of Lorton*, published in 1913 by Börje Brilioth. Brilioth was a Swedish linguist based in Uppsala, and I dispute some of his analysis of the development of the dialect later in this volume, but his recordings of the phonology of the dialect have been invaluable.

In addition to this, we have the detailed recordings acquired by researchers in the 1950s and early 1960s as part of the Orton dialect survey. These recordings are what I will use to paint a picture of the phonology of Cumbrian on the cusp of significant southern influence. I will closely analyse a few example sentences, bearing in mind that there will be differences in pronunciation between geographic areas of Cumbria. I will follow each sentence with an IPA transcription, and then a brief analysis of anything in it of note. The sentences selected will be conversational and relatively rapid. The first sentence was spoken by Isaac Brown, a resident of Brigham, in 1954. Brown was born in 1875.

> I don't know whether she - they o' come out, or not, but she- they come out on her hand. If it hed been hatched in t'nest, maybe an- er, one or two eggs hedn't hatched, you see, it would never have been known.

[ɐɾɵːʔ nɒː ˈwɜðə ʃiː - ðə ɒː kʊm aʊt ə nʊt bɒt ʃɵ - dɵ kɒm ɒʊt ɒn ɜɾ hɐnd. ɪf ɪt ɜd bɪn ɐʔtʃt ɪnʔ nest, ˈmɛbɪ ɜn- ɜː wɑn ɜ tɒʊ ɛgz ɛd.nt hɐʔtʃt, jɜ seɪ, ɪt wɵd ˈnɪvɵɾ bɪn nɔːn]

Now, this is a narrow transcription closely following Brown's actual speech, so it is certainly not a good representation of his underlying phonology. When speaking quickly, people often speak imprecisely, pronouncing things with as minimal effort as possible while still making their meaning known, emphasising the odd word which is pronounced with the full values of its phonemes. For example, the enunciation of *known* as [nɔːn] correlates with what I would expect from a Cumbrian speaker of this era, and the word is stressed within the sentence, being pronounced for longer and with a higher pitch than the surrounding words.

The feature here that is most widespread in the north of England is the reduction of the definite article - the word *the* - to something like /t/, or a glottal stop. This is rendered in various ways in writing, which I will discuss in more detail later. The speaker here uses a glottal stop affixed not to the beginning of the word the definite article applies to (in this case *nest*), but the end of the previous word. This is common in dialects where this form of the definite article occurs.

In terms of phonology - some vowels are consistent throughout. The short vowel in the *hand* lexical set is regularly /ɐ/. That in the *come* set is regularly /ʊ/. In the *if* set, it is /ɪ/, although noticeably tenser than in standard English. In the *nest* set, it falls somewhere halfway between /e/ and /ɛ/, and it is often difficult to decide on which of those two IPA characters to use. The *house* vowel is /ɒʊ/, the *see* vowel is /eɪ/. The central vowel, probably best characterised as deviations from schwa /ə/, varies in quality from /ɜ/ to /ɵ/, apparently depending on its surroundings. It's worth noting that both are slightly fronted.

Mr Brown varies between dropping and pronouncing /h/ sounds at the starts of words, a phenomenon well-recorded in many dialects in 19th- and early 20th-century England. Whether he's speaking quickly or enunciating has no bearing on whether or not he drops /h/. Elsewhere in the same recording, he sometimes affixes an initial /h/ to words that would not have it in standard English (*egg* becomes *hegg*). Again, this is done variously, as though the /h/ is optional.

Anecdotally, my own grandfather, born in 1936, exhibits this feature as well, occasionally saying *hegg* rather than *egg*.

O' is the Cumbrian cognate of the English word *all*. This is regular, and will be explained later.

Mr Brown speaks partially rhotically, not pronouncing the /r/ at the end of *whether*, but pronouncing it in *her* and *never*. My grandfather would follow a similar pattern.

/s/ is pronounced with the tongue slightly further back than it would be in standard English.

Finally, he uses *come* as the past tense of *come*, rather than *came*. Levelling of the past and present tense happens in some words in Cumbrian, but does not seem to be a regular feature of the dialect.

The second sentence is part of a recording made at Threlkeld, also in 1954, and features a Mrs Mills, born in 1883.

> Mak a wohl in t'middle... put a bit o' salt around, you kna... and put a, er... crummel your yeast in... and mek it just look... new milk warm, they used to reckon water had to be for yeast, you know... and than you'd... worked it up... wid flour... and, er... just this in't middle, worked it up, and than you lea- left it, er, to rise up. And efter it gat risen to t'top, well you... set to wark to knead it. Mix it o' up togider in your... your tin of watter, you know. Warm. Nut owwer het.

> [mak ɜ wɔːl ɪnʔ ˈmiˌɾl... pʊɾɜbiɾɜ sɔlt ɜˈɹəʊnd, jɜ nɐː... ɜn pʊt ɜðɜ, ɛː... ˈkɹɪmɜl jɜ jɛst ɪn... mɛk ɪt d͡ʒɜs lʊuk... njʊː mɪlk waːm, ðɪ jʊustɜ ˈɹæxɜn ˈwɛtɜɾ ɪd tɜ bɪː fɜɹ jɪst, jɜ nɔː. n... nan jɜ... wʊkt ɪt

ʊp... wɪd ˈflʌwɜɾ... ɜn, ɜː... d͡ʒəst ðɪs ɪnt ˈmɪɾl,
wʊkt ɪt ʊp, ɜn ðan je lɪj- left ɪt, ɜ, tɜ ɾɐiz ʊp. ɜn
ˈɛftɜɾ ɪt jats ˈɹɪzɜn tɜt tɒp, wɜl jɜ... sɪt tɜ wɐɾk tɜ
niid ɪt. mɪks ɪt ɒː ʊp tɜˈgɪðɜɹ n jɜ... jɜɾ tɪn ɜ
ˈwɐtɜɾ, jɜ nɔː... wɐʌm... nʊt ˈɐʊwɜɾ et]

Mrs Mills does more pronouncedly what Mr Brown does a
couple of times, which is to turn /d/ into an alveolar tap /ɾ/
between vowels when speaking rapidly. Otherwise, she uses
very similar vowels to Mr Brown, though occasionally realising
the *if* vowel as /i/. Her *house* vowel is /ʊu/ - the same as it was
throughout most of southern England just after the great vowel
shift. This is a point of particular interest that I will revisit later.
She does not always aspirate word-initial voiceless plosives /p/,
/t/ and /k/, as most modern speakers would. In many regards, she
speaks rapidly and imprecisely, and this recording is very useful
in getting an idea of the allophonic ranges of her phonemes.

The third sentence is from Gosforth, recorded again in 1954, and
is spoken by a Mr Sim, born in 1887.

These fellas about here what gaas to t'fell, you know,
they'll go with these big heavy shoes, like, they'll get
them made o' t'purpose to ga to the fell, like.

[ðeɪz ˈfɛlɜz əˈbəʊt ˈhɪː wət gæs tɜʔt fɛl, jɜ nɑ,
ðɜ... ðəl ɣɒː ðɪs bɪg ˈɛvei ʃəʊz, leɪk ð gɪʔt ðɜm
mɛd ðɜ ˈpɚpəsɪ gæː tə ðə fɛl, leɪk]

Mr Sim exhibits many traits already mentioned, alongside a
couple of other interesting quirks of pronunciation. For one
thing, his /z/ and /s/ sounds are pronounced with the tongue
further back in the mouth than they would be in standard
English, nearer the hard palate. Elsewhere in the recording, he
pronounces /tr/ clusters with a dental /t/ and a tapped /r/ - that is,
[t̪ɾ]. This is recorded on numerous occasions in the written

volumes of the Orton survey.

In one period of rapid speech, he realises the /g/ phoneme in *ga* ('go') as the fricative [ɣ]. Though this is tantalisingly similar to the kind of allophonic variation found in Old English and Proto-Germanic, it may be an irregularity, as he later pronounces /g/ as the usual plosive between two voiced sounds.

The sentence is interesting from a grammatical point of view. He says the equivalent of *these fellas about here what goes to the fell,* rather than the more standard *these fellas around here that go to the fell.* In Cumbrian, *about* is used more generally than *around,* so this word choice is unsurprising. *What* is used as a conjunction to begin a new clause, where *that* would be used in standard English. It is used in weak form with the unstressed vowel /ə/, which is normal for conjunctions in English (and other Germanic languages).

Mr Sim also has the habit, found elsewhere in the far north of England, of putting the word *like* at the end of clauses as a filler, or a way of indicating that the clause is finished.

For the plural form of *to go* (Cumbrian *ga, gan*), Sim has *gaas.* This is in line with a broader levelling of verb conjugation found in Cumbrian, although there are still underlying rules which differ slightly from those of standard English. Nonetheless, this chapter is about phonology and I'll avoid tangents.

The next recording is of Bill Ewing, born 1897, and was recorded in Great Strickland in 1955:

> Beests, when they lig down, sometimes catches their knees on them, and you get beests with big knees. But I don't think that big knees are otogither... bla... should o... be otogither blamed on that, because they... they run hand-in-hand with abortions, chiefly.

> [bəɪs wɪn ðɜ lɪg dʒʊn ˈsʊmtaːmz ˈkætʃɪðɜ nəɪz ɒn ðɜm ɜn jɜ jɪt bəɪs wəd bɪg nəɪz.
> bɜɾɐ dʊn θɪŋk ðət bɪg nəɪz ɜɾ ˌɒtɪˈgɪðɜɾ... blɛ...
> ʃʊd ˌɒ... bɪ ˌɒtɪˈgɪðɜɾ

blɛɐmd ən ðɐt bɪ'çəs ð̪ɜ... ð̪ɜ ɹʊn hɐnd in hɐnd
wɪd ɜ'bɔːʃɪnz 'tʃəɪfləɪ]

This is the first Westmorland speech we have examined, and it
shows a couple of as-yet-unseen realisations; the *see* vowel is
realised as [əɪ], common throughout Cumbria nowadays, and the
blame vowel is [ɛɐ]. The *if* vowel sits right on the boundary
between [ɪ] and [i], frequently crossing that boundary in my
opinion. Elsewhere in the recording, Ewing shows that his *bet*
vowel is [e], distinct from the *if* vowel. The *time* vowel is
monophthongal, being [aː] here; this is a common feature in
other parts of northern England, and will come into play later.
The word *o'* ('all') is realised as something halfway in rounding
between [ɒ] and [ɑ]. The phonemes /s/ and /z/ are very backed,
as they are in Mr Sim's recording. Schwa is almost always
realised as [ɜ], which is becoming a common theme.
Another commonality with Mr Sim's recording is the realisation
of word-initial /g/ as a fricative in certain phonological contexts.
In this case I've transcribed it as [j] as the start of *get* when
immediately preceded by a word ending in a vowel. This is only
heard to happen in rapid speech.
The phoneme /r/ is pronounced as a tap [ɾ], an approximant [ɹ],
and something in-between - possibly a tap with lip rounding. It is
occasionally pronounced post-vocalically.
Albert Davidson, born 1879, was recorded in Hunsonby in 1953:

> When I went to skiul, we hed sort of a… rather a fussy
> old sort of a skiulmaister, he wasn't a bad skiulmaister
> [???]. He used to hev some peculiar ideas, you know.

> [wɜn ɐ: wɪnt tə skxɪəl wɪ hed 'söːɾəvɜ... 'ɾɛːðɜɾ ɜ
> 'fʊsɪ ɒːld söːt əv ə 'skxɪəlˌmɛːstɜɾ, ɪ 'wɛzn̩t ɜ bɐd
> 'skxɪəlˌmɛːstɜɾ [???], ɪ'jʊustɜ... ɛ sʊm
> pə'kjʊulɪjˌɜɾ ˌɐɪ'diːˌɜz, jɜ nɒː]

This is the first sentence that gives us a realisation of the *school*, *book* vowel, which is [ɪə]. It also shows very clearly something which is on the cusp of happening in some of the other recordings; a process called **affrication**, where a plosive consonant like /t/, /k/ or /p/ 'drags on' a bit longer, so that it sounds like a plosive followed by a fricative articulated in the same place. This happens to the /k/, which becomes [k͡x]. This process has also affected Scouse accents, leading to the stereotype of Liverpudlians pronouncing /k/ sounds with a fricative at the back of the throat. This also happens to /t/ sounds in some Cumbrian (and Scouse) speech.

Affrication has the potential to go further; standard German is a good example of where a system of plosives has become a system of either affricates or fricatives. The word *to* in English is cognate with, and used in roughly the same way as, the word *zu* in German. The English word is pronounced /tu:/ in an RP accent, the German word /t͡su:/. They both come from the Proto-Germanic word **tō*, but the English word has retained the initial plosive consonant, and the German word has affricated it, dragging it out so that it ends with a fricative /s/ sound.
In some cases, German has removed the initial plosive altogether, resulting in words like *Wasser* and *Pfeffer,* cognate with *water* and *pepper* in English.
This is an example of something that might be called 'lazy' or 'slurred' speech in one language[3], but has become part of standard pronunciation in another. Sound change is a continuous process affecting all languages and dialects, and a lot of sound change is driven by people finding less energy-costly ways of pronouncing things. There is not one person today whose native language is not the product of their predecessors economising on pronunciation.

---

[3] It is vital to note that these are not words used by linguists, as they make unnecessary and negative value judgments about speech.

The earliest recording of a Cumbrian speaker I have been able to find is from the Berliner Lautarchiv British and Commonwealth Recordings, and was collected by Wilhelm Doegen in 1917. The speaker is only 27, having been born in 1890, around the same time as a lot of the British Dialect Survey participants. However, its earlier recording date means that his pronunciation is less likely to have been affected by outside influences.

Doegen had people read a Bible passage with as close to the exact same wording as possible in order to provide the most reliable comparison of regional accents, so this is not a good source of dialect words, only pronunciation. The man's name was Thomas Jackson.

> There was a man who had two sons. T'younger of them said til his father, 'Give me that part of your goods that belangs to me.' So the father gave him his share. Not many days afterwards, t'young man gathert together all his belangings and went away into a far country.

[ði:ɾ wɒz ə mɐn huw'ɛd twɛː sonz. 'tjʊŋɡɜ ˌɾɐv ðɛm sɛd tɪl ɪz 'fɛːðɜɾ, ɡɪv mɪ ðɐt pɐːʈ ɐv jɜɾ ɡʊdz ðɐt bɪ'lɐŋs tɜ mɪː. sɔʊ ðɜ 'fɐðɜ ɡɛːv ɪm ɪz ʃɛːɾ. nʊt 'mɪnɪ dɛːz 'ɐftɜwʊdz, tjʊŋ mɐn 'ɡɐðɜʈ tɜ'ɡɪðɜɾ ɔːl ɪz bɪ'lɐŋɪŋs ɐ wɪnt ɜ'wɛː 'ɪntʊu ɜ fɐɾ 'kʊntɾiː]

He enunciates reasonably clearly. He realises /r/ much more consistently word-finally, pronouncing it in almost all words where it occurs in spelling. He realises etymological /r/ in the word *part* by pronouncing retroflex [ʈ] afterwards, rather than the usual [t]. In the word *country*, despite the poor recording quality, it is clear that he dentalises the /t/ before an alveolar tap, as indicated by Brilioth and seen in the Orton survey.

Having made some observations about the phonetic realisations of particular sounds, most of which directly agree with things recorded in the written volumes of the Orton survey, we can piece together a broad and accurate phonology of Cumbrian at a particular point in history, going into some detail about the phonetic realisations of phonemes. Most of the participants in the Orton survey were (deliberately) over the age of 60, having been born in the late 19th century. The other piece of literature I mentioned, Brilioth's *Grammar of the Lorton Dialect*, was written in 1913, and although it is specific to a particular parish and may not reflect wider trends, it goes into a lot of detail about the phonemes of Cumbrian and the lexical sets into which its vocabulary is divided. For the sake of a round number, it doesn't seem unreasonable to imagine that the phonology I'm about to describe probably applied in 1900.

The short vowels were as follows:

/ɐ/ - *man, ran, gan*
/e/ - *plet, forset, net*
/ɪ/ - *wit, ling, bit*
/ɒ/ - *rot, loft, rok*
/ʊ/ - *mun, gun, sun*
/ə/ - *abuut, aback, watter*

I will use these characters in broad transcriptions throughout the book, although the phonetic realisations may vary. In 1900:

/ɐ/ may have been realised as [ɐ] or [a].
/e/ may have been realised as [e], [ɛ] or [ɪ], or anywhere on the spectrum between those three qualities.
/ɪ/ may have been realised as [ɪ] or [i]. In either case, it was markedly less centralised than RP /ɪ/. There may have been cases where /ɪ/ and /e/ overlapped, and some speakers may have had them merged. This will be discussed later.
/ɒ/ was usually [ɒ].
/ʊ/ was usually [ʊ]. varying in exact quality between speakers and depending on the surrounding sounds.
/ə/ was fronted, usually [ɜ] but occasionally [ɔ] depending on surrounding sounds.

The lexical sets of Cumbrian short vowels overlap significantly with those of RP English, but there are a lot of cases where they do not. This includes words like *never* and *not*, which normally take the next highest vowel (in terms of articulation) to the one they would take in standard English, so that *not* is *nut* [nʊt] and *never* is *nivver* [ˈnɪvɛɾ]. These are difficult to explain developmentally. Many examples of non-overlap between RP and Cumbrian are very easy to explain, and actually reflect Cumbrian being more conservative than RP.

The long vowels are as follows:

/ɐː/ - *sark, warm, barn*
/ɛː/ - *day, leik, bleik*
/iː/ - *reet, need, neet*
/ɔː/ - *koaf, wo, fo*
/uː/ - *hus, mus*

A couple of these are rather more difficult, and could reasonably be transcribed differently.

/ɐː/ could be [ɐː] or something approaching [aː].
/ɛː/ could be [ɛː] or something approaching [eː], with a leaning towards the former.
/iː/ could be [iː]. Alternatively, as the century progressed, it could have been diphthongal [ɪi] or [əɪ], or occasionally [eɪ].
/uː/ could be [uː], or diphthongal [ʊu] or [əʊ].
/ɔː/ could be [ɔː] or a markedly unrounded [ɒː].

Even these are generalisations, and I will make clarifications on these as the book progresses. In the cases of /iː/ and /uː/, they are recorded as monophthongal in some speakers as late as the 1950s, but had certainly started to break in Brilioth's time. He remarks that the *house* vowel is in the early stages of a diphthongisation process, and this process has completed in most modern older Cumbrian speakers (whether or not it has completed in younger speakers is a bit of a moot point, as their phonology is heavily influenced by outside dialects). Brilioth records some long vowels that can only exist in light of non-rhoticity, and for the sake of neatness, I will count these as being the realisation of a phonemic vowel-consonant cluster, presuming the rhotic to still be present as a phoneme even if it is not realised by non-rhotic speakers in most situations. Note also that words in the *koaf* set can be realised with an /ɐl/ cluster; again, I will discuss this in depth later.

The diphthongs are as follows:

/ɐɪ/ - *time, like, bite*
/ɐʊ/ - *nowt, Lowther, stower*
/ɒɪ/ - *boil, toil, oil*

There was, and is, defined regional variation within modern Cumbria in terms of the realisation of the first diphthong:

/ɐɪ/, in the north and east of modern Cumbria, could be [ɛɪ] or [eɪ]. In parts of Westmorland it could be [ɐ:]. In other places, a realisation of [ɐɪ] was commonplace.
/ɐʊ/ could be [ɐʊ] or [ɒʊ].
/ɒɪ/ was usually [ɒɪ].

There is also a series of rather more complicated 'diphthongs': complicated both because they are not always diphthongs, and because from the perspective of RP English, they represent a drastic mangling of lexical sets:

/jɐ/ - *yan, yat, steann, beann*
Word-initially, this is always realised as [jɐ]. In the middle of a word, it may be [jɐ], [iɐ], [eə], [ɛə] or [ɛɐ]. It could probably occur word-finally as [eə], but in Brilioth's speakers, it seems to have been realised word-finally as [ɪə] or [iə], placing it in the *book* lexical set (see below). In varieties that make a distinction between the word-initial and other environments, that distinction is probably phonemic, and may be recorded as such in this book when referring to those particular speakers.

/jʊ/, /ɪə/ - yubm, yuf, biuk, niuk, twee
Word-initially, this is always [jʊ]. In the middle of a word or
word-finally, it may be [jʊ], [iʊ], [ɪʊ], [iə] or [ɪə], or occasionally
[ɪː] or [iː]. In the middle of a word, this is more likely to be a
diphthong than a semivowel-vowel cluster. This is more likely to
be the pattern in this lexical set than it is in the *yan* set.

/wɔː/ - wohl, cwol, mworning
This is probably [wɔː] or [wɒː] regardless of its whereabouts in
the word. On the face of it, it is rather less complicated than the
other two.

The consonants and consonant clusters of Cumbrian are also
divergent from those of RP English, though perhaps having more
in common with other conservative northern English and
Scottish dialects. The voiceless plosives are /p/, /t/ and /k/. They
may be affricated to some degree as [pɸ], [ts] and [kx] in certain
positions, although the fricative element is generally short. This
affrication is more likely to happen in **coda position** (after a
vowel, at the end of a syllable).
In RP English, voiceless plosives before stressed vowels are
aspirated unless they are preceded by /s/. In Cumbrian, they may
be aspirated or unaspirated. In other positions, the aspiration
pattern is as it would be in RP.
The voiced plosives are /b/, /d/ and /g/, and these do not tend to
be affricated as far as I can tell, although we have seen that /g/
can become a voiced fricative in rapid speech in certain
phonological environments, for example when situated between
two other voiced sounds.
The voiceless fricatives /f/, /s/, /θ/ and their voiced equivalents
/v/, /z/ and /ð/ are as in RP, although /s/ and /z/ are realised
further back towards the palate.
The phoneme /r/ is realised in a number of ways, chiefly as an
alveolar tap [ɾ], and may not be realised at all when not pre-
vocalic. I would strongly suggest, given Scottish and other
northern English trends and Brilioth's remarks about the
consistency of /r/ in his time, that this disappearance of /r/ in

coda position is recent and a result of southern influence, and there are numerous older speakers today who pronounce /r/ in coda position as a tap.

In Mrs Mills' speech, /r/ is realised as an alveolar tap in syllable onset (whether on its own or in a cluster), intervocalically and postvocalically. It is occasionally realised as an approximant (as in standard English) when word-initial or intervocalic, but never word-finally. My grandfather's speech agrees with this pattern. A brief trill may occur word-finally. At times, Mrs Mills pronounces intervocalic /r/ as something which sounds a bit like a uvular fricative, as in parts of the north-east, but I do not trust my ears here; I have never heard this realisation in any living speaker or seen it described by any grammarian, so this might just be a peculiarity of her own pronunciation, an artefact of the recording equipment or my ear not being very good. Throughout the 20th century, it seems to have been steadily replaced by the alveolar approximant [ɹ] widespread in other English varieties, probably as a result of outside influence. Brilioth's *Grammar* shows the first signs of non-rhoticity creeping into Cumbrian; by his reckoning, a rhotic was realised in most environments in 1913. However, where it occurred after a stressed vowel and before an alveolar plosive such as /t/ or /d/, it disappeared, instead affecting the plosive in a way Brilioth describes like this:

> *'Superdental gum-stop-breath, like the combination* rt *in Swedish* hjärta. *'*

This presumably refers to voiceless and voiced retroflex plosives [ʈ] and [ɖ], which is indeed how he transcribes them. The corresponding fricatives /s/ and /z/ can also be retroflex in this environment: [ʂ] and [ʐ]. When /r/ immediately follows /t/ or /d/, the plosive becomes dental.

The sonorant nasals [m], [n] and [ŋ] are pronounced the same as in RP English, although the [ŋg] clusters found in RP are rare or non-existent because of a rule whereby an original nasal-plosive cluster between a stressed and an unstressed vowel loses its plosive, so that *finger* is [ˈfɪŋɜɾ], *longer* is [ˈlɒŋɜɾ] etc.

The sonorant /l/ is 'clear' and unvelarised in all environments, as in standard German. Unlike in RP, there is no velarisation of this consonant in coda position.

/h/ may be dropped at the beginnings of words, but was frequently added to them in cases of what might be **hypercorrection**. For readers unfamiliar, hypercorrection happens when a person deliberately applies rules they believe to be a sign of higher social status or education, but over-applies them to words that are not normally affected. An example of this already covered here is that of *egg* becoming *hegg*.

Words in southern English are affected by something called **glottal reinforcement**, where a glottal stop is inserted between a vowel and a plosive consonant in coda position, so that *stop* is [stɒʔp]. This does not occur in Cumbrian. Even many broader younger speakers today do not exhibit glottal reinforcement, although many now do as a result of outside influence.

For the sake of having it in a nice chart, then, the vowel inventory of later Cumbrian looks like this:

i	ɪ		ʊ	u
e				o
		ə		
ɛ				ɔ
				ɒ
		ɐ		

The Germanic languages tend to be very large in terms of vowel inventories, having between 8 and 17 phonemic vowels, so 11 is by no means unusual. Given that the underlying phonology of the consonants is very similar to that of RP, with the only differences being in realisation and allophonic range, I see no need to put them into a chart.

Finally, the **phonotactic** rules of later Cumbrian are slightly different from those of standard English. A language's phonotactic rules govern what sounds are allowed to occur in what sequences. For example, standard English contains the phonemes /s/ and /p/, and it allows a sequence like /sp-/ (as in *spin*), but it does not allow a sequence like /ps-/. It also doesn't allow sequences like /fp-/ or /ɹg/.

Later Cumbrian is largely the same, with the following notable exceptions (and possibly some others, depending on the specific variety and time period):

- A syllable **onset**[4] can, in theory, contain any consonant followed by /j/, which is not allowed in standard English. This is usually followed by either /ɐ/ or /ʊ/. Consider *steann* ('stone') /stjɐn/; *beann* ('bone') /bjɐn/.

- Contrary to the above rule, for some speakers, an onset with /hj/ is not allowed. Words that have this sequence in standard English will just have /j/ for these speakers.

- In broad later Cumbrian, /ŋg/ clusters are not allowed in any position. /-nd-/ and /-mb-/ clusters are not allowed in the middle of a word, and for some speakers, are not allowed in any position at all.

---

[4] The syllable onset is the sequence of sounds, almost always consonants, at the start of a syllable.

Beests when the lig down

Some times catches their knees on them

And you get beests wid big knees

Intonation — the
rise and fall of
the speaker's voice.

Development of the Short Vowels.

The development of the short vowels from Northumbrian Old English to later Cumbrian is perhaps even less eventful than it is in RP English, and will not take up much space. The exact qualities of the short vowels of Old English are inaccessible, but we can certainly get within a couple of IPA characters. In any case, none have changed dramatically in Cumbrian. Northumbrian Old English had an inventory of short vowels something like this:

    i y   u
    e ø   o

    æ   ɑ

By the middle English period, /ø/ had unrounded and merged with /e/, and /y/ had unrounded and merged with /i/. Short /æ/ and /ɑ/ had merged together. I will write this phoneme as /ɐ/ from that point onwards because that is how I represent it in later Cumbrian, and it is perfectly possible that this was the phonetic quality in north-western Middle English as well. By about 1400, then, we have something like this:

    i   u
    e   o
        ɐ

Structurally, this is extremely similar to the later Cumbrian short vowel inventory. Given that we do not know whether short vowels in Old English had exactly the same qualities as their long vowels, and we do know that later Cumbrian did/does not, we could alternatively reconstruct the short vowels of northern Middle English like this:

ɪ   ʊ

ɛ   ɔ

        ɐ

Of these two systems, I would be more inclined towards the former, assuming that a short vowel closely corresponded in quality to a long vowel. This makes cases of open-syllable lengthening (which will be covered later) easier to explain and describe, as they only require a change in length, rather than one in both length and quality.

In either case, there is little change in quality from early Middle English to later Cumbrian, and no chain shift of lexical sets as there is in the long vowels. My account of the changes here largely agrees with Brilioth's.

Note that where I say a vowel 'corresponds with RP', I imply that it comes by the expected Old or Middle English route unless otherwise stated.

/ɐ/ corresponds closely with RP /æ/ in words like *cat, trap, bat, matter*. Its lexical set extends further, encompassing other words that had /æ/ or /ɑ/ in Old English; this includes words such as *what* /wɐt/, *swan* /swɐn/, *water* /'wɐtər/, *father* /'fɐdər/, *make* /mɐk/, *take* /tɐk/, *ladle* /'lɐdl/ which have taken other vowels in RP. Note that this lexical set only includes reflexes of Old English /æ/ where it occurred before a nasal consonant, or in syllables that were **open** in Old English where the next syllable contained /r/ or /l/[5].

---

[5] An **open** syllable is one that does not end in a consonant sound. This can be obvious, like in the words *go* and *snow* in standard English, or it can be less obvious, like in the word *water*. Open syllables can be difficult to identify because there are situations where clusters of consonants exist between syllables, and the line between the syllables is hard to place - for example, in the word *gangrene*. As a rule of thumb, assume that consonants are part of the **onset** (start) of a syllable wherever possible, if that does not break the phonotactic rules of the language.

/e/ corresponds to RP /ɛ/ in words like *wet, set, health, flesh, meddle, vessel*, but extends to instances of Old English /æ/ that did not join the *cat* lexical set (see above). See *efter* ('after') /ˈɛftər/, *gev* ('gave') /gɛv/, *kest* ('cast') /kɛst/, *wesh* ('wash') /wɛʃ/.

/i/ corresponds to RP /ɪ/ in words like *bit, stitch, brig* ('bridge'), *dwinnel* ('dwindle'), *spinnel* ('spindle'), *filth, wish* and *list*. It extends to *find* [fɪnd] and *wind* ('to wind') [wɪnd], where in RP has taken a form with a Middle English long vowel.

It is also found in words containing the root *ever*, such as *never* and *every* ([ˈɪvər], [ˈɪvriː], [ˈnɪvər]), and the seldom-found preposition *iv* (cognate with English 'of'). The former is a reflex of Old English long /æː/, the latter of short /æ/. These must be presumed to be early borrowings from a neighbouring dialect, given their irregularity.

/ɒ/ corresponds to RP /ɒ/ in words like *cross, box, otter, fodder* ('feed'), *soft, coffin*. It extends to instances of Old English /o/ in open syllables such as *brokken* ('broken') /ˈbrɒkən/, *frozzen* ('frozen') /ˈfrɒzən/, *spokken* ('spoken') /ˈspɒkən/.

/u/ corresponds with both the *put* and *strut* lexical sets in RP, which significantly overlapped in Middle English but split apart in southern English speech. This is a common feature of northern English dialects. Bear in mind that this correspondence can not be applied across-the-board, because a lot of words which in RP are now in the *put* lexical set (like *foot, book, rook*) come from Old English long /oː/, which developed differently in Cumbrian. In any case, /ʊ/ emerges from most instances of Old English /u/, including *pund* ('pound') /pʊnd/ and *fund* ('found') /fʊnd/ which take a different lexical set in RP. Some Old English /wi/ clusters give Cumbrian /wʊ/, such as in *swum* ('swim') /swʊm/, *whistle* /ˈwʊsəl/.

Cumbrian has a variant of the /ʊ/ phoneme in places where a lot of vowels have merged and centralised before /r/, such as in *kirk* ('church') /kʊrk/ and *nurse* /nʊrs/.

Some finer points about the quality of vowels may be gleaned from spelling evidence. You may recall me saying that in later Cumbrian, we hear a great proximity in some speakers between /e/ and /ɪ/. In some speakers, both can be realised as [ɪ], and the phonemes could be argued to have merged in all environments. Note that this almost always involves the /e/ phoneme raising; /ɪ/ rarely moves at all.

This phenomenon can be clearly seen in various 19th-century collections of songs in the dialect, in which authors often treat the letters <i> and <e> as interchangeable in the *nit* lexical set, but invariably use <e> in the *net* set. As far as I have noticed, this goes back at least as far as the 1740s. Joseph Relph's 1747 *Miscellany of Poems*, some of which are in Cumbrian, has the name 'Betty' spelled *Betty* and *Bitty*, each numerous times. While the same situation does not exist for the back vowels, it is true that /ʊ/ is usually realised less centrally in Cumbrian than in RP.

Also pertinent is the question of **unstressed** vowels: these are vowels that occur in an unstressed syllable. In textbook Old English, these vowels probably had full, distinct realisations similar to those of short vowels in stressed syllables, and did not follow the modern German pattern of reducing most unstressed syllables to a central vowel like /ə/. However, towards the end of the Old English period, these unstressed vowels start to centralise. We know this because writers start to get them mixed up in spelling, a clue that the spoken values were starting to level as something like /ə/.

In the north-west, this probably happened in a similar way, albeit possibly starting slightly earlier, leading to the disappearance of grammatical gender in northern dialects rather earlier than in southern dialects (more on this later).

By the early modern English period in the south, we see evidence that people were reducing an awful lot of vowels to /ə/ in rapid speech, and this kind of thing is reflected in both modern broad Cumbrian and in 18th- and 19th-century texts. Most pronouns have a **strong** form and a **weak** form, something found less in standard English. The **strong** form is used when the pronoun is emphasised, whereas the **weak** form is used the rest

of the time. In the weak forms, all vowels are usually reduced to
/ə/ (like the 'uh' sound as the start of standard English *about*).

Me /miː/	Ma /mə/
Thou /ðuː/	The /ðə/
Thee /ðiː/	The /ðə/
He /hiː/	He /ə/
She /ʃiː/	She /ʃə/
They /ðɛː/	They /ðə/
Them /ðem/	'em /əm/

A very similar pattern of strong and weak pronouns is found in
Dutch, and it also applies to Cumbrian prepositions.
In addition to this, Cumbrian reduces unstressed vowels that
would not usually be reduced in standard English. The *-ow*
endings of words like *borrow, marrow, swallow* are all reduced
to /ə/, so that the words are /ˈbɒrə/, /ˈmɛrə/, /ˈswɐlə/. Endings
that in standard English contain /ɪ/ often have it as /ə/ in
Cumbrian; *coming, thinking* are /ˈkʊmən/, /ˈθɪŋkən/.
As in a lot of languages, an unstressed vowel-consonant cluster
may have the vowel elided in rapid speech, meaning that
consonants can sometimes be **syllabic** (that is, a syllable can
consist of just one consonant with no vowels), although this is
sometimes a matter of phonetic realisation and not underlying
phonology. There is occasionally a case to be made that this is
phonemic, so I will alternate between the two when transcribing
things in this book. This process applies to the word *-dale* where
it occurs unstressed at the end of a place name, for example
Ennerdale [ˈenɜrˌdl̩] or *Mosedale* [ˈmwɔːzˌdl̩]. In both of these
transcriptions, the little marking under the letter *l* shows that the
l is syllabic; it takes the place of a vowel as the **nucleus** of the
syllable. Let's look more closely at an example sentence in later
Cumbrian, first enunciated slowly, then spoken rapidly and
casually. I will make the characters bigger so that you can
examine them more closely. The sentence in standard English is
you keep to yourself. Firstly, enunciated fully in later Cumbrian:

[ðuː kiːps tɪl ðɐɪˈsel]

And then spoken at a casual, rapid pace:

[ðɜ kiːps tl ðɜˈsel]

In the second sentence, you can see that all stressed syllables, such as *keeps* and the *-sel* part of *thysel*, are still pronounced with their full vowel qualities, just as they would be when fully enunciated. However, all of the unstressed syllables, such as *thou*, *til* and the *thy-* in *thysel* are **reduced**. They take a central, short vowel. *Til* loses its vowel altogether, with the /l/ taking its place as the syllable nucleus, effectively doing the job of the vowel.

In southern standard English, there are two vowels which are broadly common in unstressed syllables: /ə/ and /ɪ/. For a large number of modern Cumbrian speakers, these are merged as /ə/, so that *bucket, casket* and *chicken* are respectively /ˈbʊkət/, /ˈkɐskət/ and /ˈtʃɪkən/, rather than /ˈbʌkɪt/, /ˈkɑːskɪt/ and /ˈtʃɪkɪn/ as in the south. The antiquity of this isn't clear, but it may not be very old: Brilioth (1913) remarks several distinct historical environments in which the unstressed vowel remains /ɪ/, but he remarks that it is 'somewhat lowered towards the e-position and sometimes hard to distinguish from /ə/.' Older writers tend to write certain unstressed vowels with <i> in words that now have it as /ə/ (for instance *brackins* ('ferns'), which is now /ˈbrɐkənz/), and it may be that this is supposed to represent extant /ɪ/. Even for speakers with the merger, there are environments in which it does not apply.

One more note on unstressed syllables: at some point in the development of Cumbrian, a process called **epenthesis** occurred. Epenthesis means that a sound appears where there wasn't one before. In this case, wherever a high vowel (such as /i/ or /u/) was followed by /r/ at the end of a word (or in a word-final consonant cluster[6]), an unstressed vowel /ə/ was inserted between them, adding an extra syllable to the word. *Theer* ('there') /ði:r/ became *theear* /ˈði:.ər/. *Oor* ('our') /u:r/ became *ooar* /ˈu:.ər/. *Bowr* ('parlour') /bɐʊr/ became *bower* /ˈbɐʊ.ər/. This affected all words that met the condition, and seems to have spread through all Cumbrian varieties.

As for the timing of this, my suspicion is that it had not happened - or at least, was not yet **phonemic** - at the time that the *Glossarium Brigantinum* was written in 1677, because it includes words such as *boort* ('to jest') and *bowr* ('parlour') with no indication in spelling that they have two syllables. Likewise, the poetic meter used by Joseph Relph in his 1747 *Miscellany of Poems*, and the spellings of certain words, suggest that words like *wear* and *there* were being pronounced with one syllable. Forms with two syllables start to appear in the 19th century, narrowing down the date of this change satisfactorily.

---

[6] A cluster of consonants occurring at the end of a word. For example, in the word *soft*, the /f/ is not at the end of the word, but it is part of the /ft/ cluster, which is at the end of the word.

Development of the Long Vowels.

The development of the long vowels in northern English is a lot more complex, and has undergone various analyses over the last hundred-or-so years.

I'll start with an issue that's been brought up a few times by philologists when they have touched on northern Middle English literature, and that is the inconsistent spellings of words in the *home* lexical set in the Ellesmere manuscript of *The Reeve's Tale*, one of Chaucer's *Canterbury Tales*. The Ellesmere manuscript was composed shortly after Chaucer's death. Some of the so-called inconsistencies found in Ellesmere also occur in the Hengwrt manuscript, which may have been written by the same scribe.

Two of the characters from *The Reeve's Tale* were said to be from *'fer in the north; I kan nat tell where'* ('far in the north; I can not tell where'), and Chaucer made a deliberate effort to show northern speech through both his spelling and his word choices. It is one of the earliest examples of somebody writing in a dialect other than their own, and is therefore valuable even in ways that a passage written by a native speaker of a northern dialect would not be. While Chaucer may employ contemporary stereotypes, these are invaluable in allowing us to determine how a southerner might have heard northern speech, interpreting it according to their own phonology.

The issue at hand is that the author of the Ellesmere and Hengwrt manuscripts seems to go a step further in 'northernising' the dialogue of these two characters, and in doing so, he spells words of the *home* lexical set with the <ee> digraph. For example, *home* is <heem>; *gone* is <geen>; *none* is <neen>. This digraph is what a southern Middle English speaker would have used to spell the phoneme /ɛː/, suggesting pronunciations of [hɛːm], [stɛːn], [gɛːn], which are at odds with spellings from texts actually written in the north of England and employing native northern vocabulary.

Philologists have been quick to dismiss this as a fluke; Tolkien himself dismissed them as 'ghost-forms' or the product of scribal confusion. Northern writers usually spelled this lexical set according to the pattern <hame>, <gane> etc., and an interpretation of this based on the relationship between orthography and pronunciation in southern Middle English would yield pronunciations of /ˈhaːm(ə)/ and /ˈgaːn(ə)/, even though these make less sense when considering modern pronunciations that must have been derived from them.

More recent authors have taken Tolkein's dismissal of these forms to be too hasty. Jeremy Smith (1994) suggests that the spellings are a southern attempt to show post-vowel-shift northern forms, and that these spellings are only perplexing if one assumes that contemporary northern English spellings represented the same sounds as their better-understood southern counterparts. They make perfect sense if one takes a different approach. In addition to Smith's analysis from a philological angle, I will try to explain some of the evidence from modern dialect forms.

Given that this is a question of phonology, and, to a lesser extent, of phonetic realisation, the **comparative method** may be applied to modern or near-modern sound systems that have their origin in the northern middle English sound system. Cumbrian has one of those sound systems; others are found in Scots and Scottish English, and the dialects of Yorkshire, Tyne & Wear and Northumberland. For speakers unfamiliar, the comparative method is a way of triangulating ancestral forms of words by looking at their descendents in a number of related languages or dialects.

In this case, we'll take the word *home* as it is in various language varieties descended from northern Middle English, the broad forms of which remain relatively untouched by southern influence:

Cumbrian	Scots	Geordie
/jɛm/	/heːm/	/jem/
/heəm/		/heəm/
/hiɛm/		

We can reconstruct a very reasonable course of development using only the descendent forms we have here. We know that the Old English form was monophthongal /ɑ:/, which fronted to either /a:/ (or perhaps /ɐ:/) in the early Middle English period. The only monophthongal variant we find in our examples is the Scots one, /he:m/, which is very close to the form suggested by the Ellesmere spellings, [hɛ:m]. To get from [hɐ:m] to [hɛ:m] requires only a very small shift in vowel quality.

This is then in the perfect position to diverge. In Scots, it stayed largely the same, possibly raising slightly. In northern English, it first broke into a centering diphthong such as [ɛə]. In Cumbrian, this went further, first broadening to [ɛɐ], then to [eɐ], then to [iɐ]. The reduction of the first element to an onglide makes [jɐ]. All of these forms are attested in some variety of Cumbrian; all, I would suggest, are more conservative variants of [jɐ].

A similar change from short /e/ to /ja/ is known to have occurred in Old Norse - twice in certain dialects (Proto-Germanic *ebnaz > O.N. *jafn*; later, *ek* > *jak*). This shows that this variety of change is not unheard of, although I should stress that the Cumbrian change cannot be a result of Norse influence; it happened long, long after the sound changes in Old Norse had completed and affects completely different lexical sets. We must be careful not to assume Scandinavian influence everywhere; it is an appealing catch-all explanation for a person examining northern and eastern dialects of English, but plenty of uniquely northern features cannot be explained in that way, and must have been a result of regular internal change.

But as I said a little while ago, vowel systems want to remain stable and tend towards symmetry, and one big change to a vowel inventory can trigger a lot of others. How does the development of the *home* set fit into the bigger picture?

I will look at the *book* set next, because it's later reflexes bear so pre-shift sound was something like [i:] or perhaps [y:]. This was retained in Scottish varieties, but in Cumbrian it broke into a centering diphthong [iə], and diversified into its many forms from there, by analogy with the *home* set.

The first literary evidence showing the outcome of the *home* and

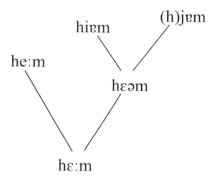

book changes comes in the 1600s, albeit not always in Cumberland or Westmorland. The 1685 text *The Praise of Yorkshire Ale* contains the spelling *yan* (one). The 1677 *Glossarium Brigantinum*, a self-styled dictionary of the Cumbrian vernacular by William Nicholson, spells words of that lexical set inconsistently; *grave* (to dig), and *geat* (path, road, way) are both pronounced /grjɐv/, /gjɐt/ by the 19th century. *A Clavis to the Foregoing Dialogue*, composed at some point between 1690 and 1730 (the dialogue in question being a

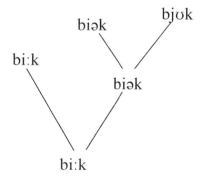

'Yorkshire dialogue') is inconsistent in its spelling of these words, just as the *Glossarium* is. It has *stone* written as *stane*, but *both* and *so* are written as *beath* and *sea* respectively. Of all the words subject to this inconsistency across both works - *grave*, *stane*, *beath* and *sea* - all would have had the same vowel, /ɑ:/, in Old English. They all still belonged to the same lexical set in the 19th century. Without strong evidence of them splitting and re-merging, I would suggest the inconsistency in spelling is just a result of people accustomed to writing in standard English not knowing quite how to transcribe the unfamiliar vowels and diphthongs of the north. It is also possible that the adoption of these shifted vowels from their origin point further north (as discussed in the chapter on Scottish influence) was messy, and did not occur in all the relevant words at once.

The writer of the *Clavis* is able to be more consistent with words in the *book* lexical set, spelling them with the trigraph ⟨ eau⟩ . *Feaut, geaud* are *foot, good* respectively. At the time it was composed, the vowel in the *meat* set in the south was /i:/, so it seems most reasonable to interpret ⟨ ea⟩ as representing the quality [i]. The trigraph in total could represent anything from /iə/ to /iu/ to /iʊ/. These timings put the change at some point prior to 1600 - roughly the time by which most of the great vowel shift had completed in the south of England.

Where either vowel was originally followed by /r/, its development has been different. In the *home* lexical set you find that Old English words like *mār* ('more') and *sār* ('sore') have become *mair* [mɛ:r] and *sair* ('sore,' 'very') [sɛ:r], their vowel quality frozen in place before the vowel broke in other words. In the *book* set you have words like Old English *mōr* ('moor'), which takes the vowel /u:/ (later Cumbrian *mooar* /'mu: ˌər/). The Old English diphthongs *ēo*, *ēa* and *īy*, as well as the long vowels *ē* and *ǣ*, have all merged as /i:/ by later Cumbrian, but the process by which they did so is difficult to unravel. My strong suspicion is that they were all merged before the great vowel shift, but a case could be (and has been) made that they were not, based on the way Brilioth sorts the lexical sets. He makes a distinction between the long vowel /iː/ and a diphthong, /eɪ/, and is very thorough in his analysis of which Old English sounds give rise to which. He says that /iː/ arises from Middle English *ih, igh* clusters, from Old English /eː/ and from /e/ before /ld/. He says that /eɪ/ (as I am transcribing it) arises from /e/ in syllables that were open in Old English, as well as *ǣ, ēo* and *ēa*. The exact value of the latter two diphthongs in Northumbrian Old English is debated; John Watson, writing in 1946, argues from spelling evidence (and from analysis of Brilioth's *Grammar*) that the two had merged by the end of the Old English period in Northumbrian. The spelling evidence, simply enough, is that authors started to mix the two up, eventually using them almost interchangeably.

His argument making use of Brilioth's work seems to be that Old English /iːy/ (usually spelled īe) gives Cumbrian /iː/, whereas Old English ēa and ēo both give Cumbrian /eɪ/. We know that in the south, Old English īe and ēo merged, producing Middle English /eː/, while ēa remained unmerged, monophthongising and eventually becoming /ɛː/. In the Early Modern English period, etymological /eː/ and /ɛː/ raised and merged as /iː/ in the *meet-meat* merger.

Watson's reasoning is that if this process had happened in Northumbrian, the original īe set could not still be separate from the ēo/ēa set by Brilioth's time; that ēo and ēa must have merged before ēo had a chance to merge with īe. I would argue that this particular argument is unravelled by the fact that īe was rare if not non-existent in Anglian dialects; the sound usually only arose through i-mutation in the south, and this i-mutation in the north produced /eː/ instead. Based on the spelling evidence he cites, though, I would accept Watson's suggestion of a merger as correct, and would say that the three sets were merged to /eː/ by the end of the Middle English period. In due course, Old English original ē and ǣ also merged into this set.

If any more confirmation is required that *meet* and *meat* have merged in later Cumbrian, Hilary Prichard conducted a study in 2014 into regional vowel realisations in the Orton survey. She found that, although Middle English /eː/ and /ɛː/ were still unmerged in some northerly parts of the midlands at the time of the survey, they were merged in the northernmost parts of England (including Cumberland and Westmorland).

I would argue that Brilioth's acknowledgement of 2 separate sets reflects the 20th-century diphthongisation process that I have already touched upon.

So we are left with these sets all merged as /eː/ by about 1200. It seems most likely for it to have retained this quality up until the start of the great vowel shift; this does not drag it into any mergers that we know not to have happened. If it had been any more open than /eː/, it would have merged with the *home* set, which it is very unlikely to have done, as the two sets are unmerged in later Cumbrian.

The final vowel is Middle English /iː/, the vowel in the *time* lexical set. In the south, this vowel remained the same from Old English to the very beginning of the great vowel shift, at which point it diphthongised. I suspect that the same was true in the north. This implies something about the order of the changes I have already described. We know that the *time* set and the *book* set are unmerged in later Cumbrian and cannot have merged before the great vowel shift, which tells us that they cannot have had the vowel /iː/ at the same time. Lass's account of the development of the *book* set has it as /yː/ before it unrounds to /iː/. In that case, the *time* set has to have moved out of that phonetic position to leave it vacant for the *book* set to unround into. I would suggest that it happened similarly in the north to the south; /iː/ became /ɪi/ became /əɪ/, and from there it diverged into its regional later Cumbrian forms, which are perhaps even more diverse than those in the *home* set.

The table overleaf shows the development of the three lexical sets, according to a model based on the simultaneous breaking of STONE and BOOK. Bear in mind that this is a hypothetical, and further discussion during this chapter will narrow down the timescale of this process further. You will notice that the three lexical sets never have the same vowel in the same stage; there are no mergers, and nor should we expect there to be, because these three vowels are not merged in later Cumbrian.

Stage 3	tɐɪm	biək	stɛɐn
Stage 2	təɪm	biək	stɛən
Stage 1	tɪim	biːk	stɛːn
ME	tiːm	byːk	stɛːn

Words like *night*, *sight* and *light* are not affected by breaking in the TIME set. In Middle English, they took a short vowel followed by a palatal consonant, as in German:

/niçt/   /siçt/   /liçt/

In the south of England, during the Middle English and Early Modern English periods, the palatal consonant disappeared. The long vowel lengthened to compensate for this disappearance, and the three words merged into the TIME set. However, in northern Middle English, the consonant never disappeared to begin with; it was retained through the great vowel shift. Two avenues of evidence tell us this. Firstly, *night* and *sight* do not have the same vowel as *time* in later Cumbrian, precluding a merger at any point in the past (/niːt/, /siːt/ but /tɐɪm/). Secondly, the palatal consonant is attested in a lot of Scottish texts, and survives in modern Scots.

A Cumbrian dialect dictionary published in 1880 by William Dickinson comments that 'formerly, even within memory,' the 'gh' sound in *night* and *sight* was pronounced as what he calls 'an aspiration.' It is likely that this describes the survival of [ç]. The sound persisted for far longer in some Scottish dialects, even being attested today. It isn't far-fetched, therefore, to put a placeholder date of around 1800 for the disappearance of the fricative, in Cumbrian, which probably varied slightly depending on location.

Brilioth records the *night* set as distinct from the *see* set in 1913, but as I have said, I think that the two sets were merged throughout the post-medieval period, and that this separation is an early sign of the 20th century diphthongisation.

It is the compensatory lengthening in the *night* set that leads me to suspect that the vowel quality was /i/ well into the Early Modern period, rather than /ɪ/; the two have slightly different qualities, and lengthening of /ɪ/ would produce /ɪː/, not /iː/. It is remotely possible that /ɪː/ came first, merging with /iː/ later, but I think it requires fewer assumptions to propose a length distinction between /iː/ and /i/ until perhaps as late as 1800, albeit with /i/ being realised slightly laxer. In fact, what I have so far analysed as /ɪ/ in later Cumbrian is often realised so tensely that it could just as well be analysed as short /i/.

Two Middle English diphthongs are notable here: those in *way* and *day*. These are normally transcribed /wej/ and /daj/, but I will transcribe them narrowly as [wei] and [dai] here because of their later developments.

Some evidence from Scotland, given in the chapter on Scottish influence, suggests that the *way* and *day* sets may have been unmerged in some places into the 1600s, with *day* smoothing to /dɛː/ and *way* remaining [waɪ], which seems at odds with their Middle English qualities. It is possible to analyse this change as being consistent with the overall vowel shift, as I will show later in the book.

This lexical set may or may not have included loan words from Old Norse that were originally pronounced with /ei/, such as *leika* ('to play') and *bleikr* ('dull yellow/red').

Later Cumbrian has all of these words, both in the *day* set and the *way* set, realised with long /ɛː/. The simplest explanation here seems to be that Middle English /aɪ/ raised to /ɛɪ/ and then diphthongised as /ɛː/ during the great vowel shift, with ME /ei/ then lowering to /ai/. Finally, /ai/ merged to /ɛː/, so that *day* and *way* now rhyme.

64

Stage 2	stɛən	dɛː	wɛː
Stage 1	stɛən	dɛː	wai
ME	stɛːn	dai	wei

An often-remarked-upon feature of some conservative northern English and Scottish dialects is that they preserve monophthongal /uː/. In Cumbrian, the quality of /uː/ seems to have remained extremely stable from the Old English period to the 20th century, before being affected by the 20th century diphthongisation.

It makes a lot of sense; /uː/ has historically had very little reason to change in Cumbrian. While in the south the chain shift occurred fairly symmetrically in both front and back vowels, in the north there were few back vowels to exert influence on each other, because the *book* vowel had fronted. /uː/ was almost untouched by pushing and pulling influences; the front vowels were by far the most dynamic.

Old English short *eo, ea, æ,* and *a* prior to /r/ manifest as /ɐː/ in later Cumbrian, giving words like *wark* ('work') /wɐːrk/, *stark* ('stiff') /stɐːrk/, *yard* /jɐːrd/. Spellings such as *wark* are recorded from before the great vowel shift throughout the north. Vowels of this kind before /r/ are generally thought to have been short in the south, and I see no reason to think this was different in the north; their eventual lengthening may have had something to do with the fronting and raising of long /ɐː/ in the *home* set, or it may have happened alongside the great vowel shift.

Complementing this lengthening of /ɐ/ in the *wark* set, you have a lengthening of /ɔ/ before liquids such as /r/, /l/ and /m/ in words like *thorn, scorn, morning*, producing /θɔːrn/, /skɔːrn/, /ˈmɔːrning/. This is very likely to have happened during the Middle English period, based on a number of avenues of evidence.

The first of these is to do with the sound's development through the great vowel shift. In later Cumbrian, we find the cluster /wɔ/ or /wɔː/ in this set. Joseph Relph's 1747 *Miscellany* has *forced* rendered as *fworc'd*, suggesting the change had completed by then. Early on in this research, I thought that it may have happened as a response to the appearance of the /jɐ/ and /jʊ/ clusters; a bid by the vowel inventory to restore some level of symmetry. Now, however, I strongly suspect that it was actually the vowels in the STONE and COMB sets that broke in tandem with each other, with the BOOK vowel changing later. I suspect this in light of evidence which will be discussed in the next chapter.

Given the process by which STONE and BOOK seem to have changed, it seems likely that /wɔ/ clusters emerged from a long vowel than a short one, with the intermediate stage /ɔə/. By analogy with /jɐ/ and /jʊ/ sequences, the /ɔ/ in a /wɔ/ sequence may have been short at first, leaving a vacant slot where the open-mid back long vowel had once been.

The second avenue of evidence is to do with inter-dialectal borrowing. It is not just different languages who borrow loan words from one another; neighbouring dialects do the same thing. You can spot these loan words by looking for words that are not the expected reflexes of their Old English forms. Take the recorded word *woat* ('oat'). This is derived from Old English *āte*. The Old English vowel *ā* in a syllable like this should correspond to Cumbrian /jɐ/, so why is the later form not *yat*? The most forthcoming explanation is that, in the Middle English period, northern English took *oat* /ɔːt/ as a loan word from a dialect that had a back vowel in this set, as most southern dialects did.

Oat was then subject to the change affecting /ɔː/, and became /wɔːt/. This sequence of events is supported by the widespreadness of the Cumbrian word *haver* ('oats'); if *haver* replaced the Old English *āte* as the normal word for oats, this would leave room for a descendent of *āte* to be re-incorporated as a loan word. However, the incorporation of a few stray loan words is not generally enough to produce a new lexical set in the receiving language, so it's likely that long /ɔː/ already existed in north-western Middle English. I suggest that this was in the *thorn, comb* lexical set.

Immediately post-vowel-shift, then, Cumbrian's inventory of long vowels (excluding diphthongs) looked something like this, bearing in mind that the COMB set originally had a diphthong:

    iː   uː
    ɛː
          ɐː

This inventory is asymmetrical and unstable. There are only two simple ways of stabilising it; raising /ɛː/ to merge with /iː/, or producing a backed vowel at the same height as /ɛː/ (which is to say, restoring a monophthongal /ɔː/ where the old one had diphthongised). The first option is less sustainable; it would make a lot of words identical and produce more ambiguity, something that vowel inventories tend to avoid doing. The more tenable option is the restoration of /ɔː/. There is ample spelling evidence for this restoration.

In the Middle English period, words like *all, fall, call* were pronounced with a short vowel; /al/, /fal/, /kal/ in the south, possibly more like /ɐl/, /fɐl/, /kɐl/ in the north-west. Spellings aligning with this are the norm prior to the great vowel shift. In the north, *cald* is also widespread for 'cold.'

In later varieties descended from northern Middle English, you see various different reflexes of this; on the one hand, you have /ɐː/, as in *a', fa', ca'* /ɐː/, /fɐː/, /kɐː/. On the other, you have /ɔː/, as in *o', fo', co'* /ɔː/, /fɔː/, /kɔː/. Both of these forms are found in both Scotland and northern England. More relevantly, both are found in Cumbria. The presence of both forms is suggestive of the order in which changes happened: firstly, the /l/ was deleted, accompanied by compensatory lengthening of the vowel. Secondly, the vowel shifted into the /ɔ/ position. In the case of the word *all*, the path of development was:

$$/\text{ɐl}/ \; > \; /\text{ɐ:}/ \; > \; /\text{ɔ:}/$$

The change from /ɐ:/ to /ɔ:/ did not occur if /ɐ:/ was followed by a sonorant, such as /r/ or /l/, so words like *start* and *barn* ('child') were unaffected, remaining /stɐ:rt/ and /bɐ:rn/. Even in varieties where the change has happened in its entirety, the quality /ɐ:/ in this lexical set is preserved in words such as *areet* ('alright') /ɐːˈriːt/, where /ɐ:/ has been protected from backing by the following /r/.

This doesn't explain some stray pronunciations of *all* as /ɐ:l/, even in the speech of modern Cumbrians. This issue requires further examination, but I think that the explanation on the previous page is an adequate starting point for further analysis, and certainly accounts for a lot of varieties.

Throughout a lot of Cumbrian, all words with etymological /ɐl/ clusters fall into this category; *ald* ('old') /ɔ:d/, *cald* ('cold') /kɔ:d/, *all* /ɔ:/, *fall* /fɔ:/, *wall* /wɔ:/. However, in some varieties, you get a different outcome in words where Middle English /l/ came between /ɐ/ and an alveolar plosive like /d/ or /t/; words such as *cald*, *ald* and *galt* ('boar'). These words have lost their /l/, but take a diphthong in later Cumbrian: /ɐʊ/. Original *cald* becomes /kɐʊd/, *ald* is /ɐʊd/, *galt* is /gɐʊt/.

This looks very much like a process called l-vocalisation, which is extremely common. It usually happens in places where /l/ is velarised; that is, pronounced with the body of the tongue up against the soft palate, as [ɫ]. A speaker economising in rapid speech will often not draw their tongue right back to the palate, leaving the airway slightly open and realising this sound as a backed vowel like [ʊ]. This is widespread in modern English. My own south-eastern accent velarises the /l/ phoneme in coda position, and in rapid speech I will often pronounce *cold* as [kʌʊd]. This has been formalised in Dutch: their cognate of *cold* is *koud*.

Later Cumbrian almost never velarises /l/, even in coda position, but the fact that it is clearly vocalised in these forms suggests that some Cumbrian varieties around the time of the great vowel shift did have it velarised in coda position, at least when followed by an alveolar plosive. Below is the example of the later Cumbrian word *gaut* ('boar').

$$[\text{gɐɫt}] \quad > \quad [\text{gɐʊt}]$$

In terms of dating, our earliest text in which the change has taken place is, once again, Relph's 1747 *Miscellany*, where he spells *all* as *aw'*.

As for isolating a time *before* which the vowel change cannot have been completed, we look to the *Glossarium Brigantinum* (1677), which contains the word *aamery* ('food storage area'). The *aam-* portion of the word seems to be cognate with standard English *alm*, as in 'alms for the poor.' The spelling ⟨ aa ⟩ , to me, clearly indicates /ɐ:/ rather than /ɔ:/. This allows us to say that, at some point between 1677 and the 1740s, both versions were probably in use; that is, that the change happened during that seventy-year period of time. Some speakers still have /ɐ:/ in certain words, although I have never heard it across all words in this set - generally, it is preserved before /l/.

Other instances of later Cumbrian /ɐʊ/ can easily be found. Some of these are survivals of loan words from Old Norse, such as *kowp* ('to exchange') from Old Norse *kaupa* ('to buy'), and *Lowther* (a river name) from Old Norse *lauðr* ('foam').

The Old Norse diphthong seems to have been /au/, so upon loaning into Old English, very little change seems to have happened to take it to the later Cumbrian form.

It also emerged from the Old English combinations *-oht* and *-ōht*, as in the words *owt* ('anything') /ɐʊt/, *bowt* ('bought') /bɐʊt/, *sowt* ('sought') /sɐʊt/, and from *-ōw* in words like *grow* /grɐʊ/, *stow* /stɐʊ/.

There are three words in this lexical set whose path of development I have been unable to trace: *owwer* ('over') /ˈɐʊˌər/, *bowwer* ('living room') /ˈbɐʊˌər/ and *stowwer* ('stick; post') /ˈstɐʊˌər/.

The diphthong /ɒɪ/ is rare, found exclusively in French loan words, and there is no reason to think its path of development is not the same as its standard English equivalent.

Having produced a broad skeleton of the vowel changes that led up to later Cumbrian, we are in a position to look at the causes of the changes, and perhaps be more specific in dating them. Causality in historical linguistics can be difficult to unpick, but looking at the pre-vowel-shift long vowel inventory of north-western English as it is reconstructed here, it's not difficult to see why significant change occurred:

<pre>
i: y: u:
e:
ɛ: ɔ:
        ɐ:
</pre>

The system is highly unstable, with four front vowels and only two back ones. An inventory like this is surely highly prone to significant and rapid change - even more so than the southern English long vowel system at the time, in line with suggestions that the great vowel shift in the south may have been in part due to northern influence. Jeremy Smith (1994), while not necessarily going this far, repeated a common sentiment that a great deal of the northern vowel shift seems to have been complete by 1400.

It's easy to wonder how a vowel system was driven to this level of asymmetry. It's possible that the *book* vowel fronted to /ø:/ as a response to the loss of Northumbrian Old English /ø:/ when it merged with /e:/, although the latter is evidenced much earlier than the former. Beyond that, no explanation is necessarily required. In his 1993 paper *Phonetic Symmetry in Sound Systems*, philologist Jan Tent posits that the tendency towards symmetry does not *restrict* sound change, but does *cause* it. That is to say, there is not much stopping a vowel system from drifting into asymmetry, but as the asymmetry increases, the pressure to stabilise will also increase.

I take this to be a satisfactory explanation for the steady destabilisation, and rapid re-stabilisation, of the Cumbrian long vowel system that I have shown here.

To tie up a loose end, at least two errant forms exist in several varieties of Cumbrian that are not in the lexical set we would expect them to be in; *aa* ('I') /ɐː/ and *laal* ('small') /lɐːl/. We would expect them both to be in the *time* lexical set, being pronounced /ɐɪ/ and /lɐɪl/ in south-western Cumbrian varieties and /ɛɪ/ and /lɛɪl/ in north-eastern varieties. We do find the expected forms, variously spelled *lile*, *lail* or *lyle*, in some literature throughout the later Cumbrian period, but the prevailing form from the 19th century to this day is *laal* or *la'al*. I put this down to a loaning from a dialect in which the *time* vowel smoothed to long /ɐː/, which is known to have happened in parts of Westmorland and in Lancashire. Why these two words in particular were loaned, I cannot say.

On another topic: there is some discussion in academia as to whether particular dialects of English actually have **phonemic vowel length**. By phonemic vowel length, I mean vowel length that actually makes a difference within the language - in every language, the lengths for which particular vowels are held will differ from speaker to speaker and from situation to situation, but do you have scenarios where two words are different from each other solely because one has a short vowel and the other has a long vowel? This is the question of phonemic vowel length. Many - perhaps most - would argue that most US varieties of English do not have phonemic vowel length, because you never have a situation where two words are differentiated only by vowel length. There is always something else differentiating them, for example, vowel quality. There are rules within US English about which vowels ought to be pronounced longer and which ought to be pronounced shorter, but this can always be gleaned from the vowel's surroundings or its quality, so this does not represent phonemic vowel length.

Some would extend this to argue that British English does not have phonemic vowel length either. I would argue that there are certain pairs of words within my idiolect that are differentiated only by their length, for example *Ken* /kɛn/ and *cairn* /kɛːn/. Vowel length in British English is also predictably based on etymology, rather than the environment in which a vowel sits. I would make the case here that vowel length was absolutely phonemic in later Cumbrian, and that numerous minimal pairs could be produced on the basis of vowel length alone. *Fen* and *fain*, *beck* and *bake*, *let* and *lait*. In certain people's idiolects, pairs such as *sop* and *soap* may also be minimal pairs. In non-rhotic later Cumbrian, there may be minimal pairs such as *ban* and *barn*.

I mentioned in my foreword that there is evidence of varieties of Cumbrian that deviated significantly from the mainstream that I describe here, having remained extraordinarily conservative into the late 1700s. The dialogues of Agnes Wheeler, an excerpt from which is included in the selected readings as the end of the book, are an excellent record of one of these varieties, and this book would be incomplete without a summary of its features, the most interesting of which are to do with the long vowels.

The vowel in the *day* lexical set seems to have avoided monophthongisation, and is still something like /ɐɪ/ in 1790, hinted at by the rhyming of *haait* ('have it') and *say't* ('say it') in her *A Song*.

Words in the *sake* lexical set are spelled with <aa>, suggesting a pronunciation something like /sɐːk/. This is similar to the pre-vowel-shift pronunciation of this lexical set in the south, and doubtless in parts of the north as well. This did not apply to words like *mean* ('moan'), which seems to have been somewhere along the mainstream course of development in Wheeler's dialect. Finally, words in the *book* set are spelled with <ea>, which is the same digraph as Wheeler uses to render the preposition *i* ('in'), suggesting a quality something like /iː/, although if the vowel was something like /iᵊ:/ or even /iə/, the spelling would still make sense.

It could even be hypothesised that Wheeler's dialect was a continuation of what was typical for most Cumbrians up until the great vowel shift, and that the course of development I have described in this chapter was limited to north-eastern Cumbria or northern Scotland, only spreading downwards into other corners of Cumbria during the 1600s. This interpretation has some support from spellings in the *stone* lexical set in 15th-century Cumbrian indentures, and it could absolutely hold water.

ARoper
war her
Potter's mark.

My grandmudder med laal hewlet whistles  oot o clay. She'd gitten t'idea frae anidder potter whose neam aa knān't.

T'whistle bit were anonder t'tail. This'en is aboot two inch to; a laal bit bigger nor this picture. Aa olas think o' hulets when aa think on her. She said til me, she liked t'thowt at fwoke wad ya day dig up her pots lang efter she'd liggen low.

Development of the Consonants.

The finer details of the development of consonants - those surrounding the slight backing of /s/ or the slight affrication of /k/, for instance - are often inaccessible to philologists, and I will discuss this point further at the end of this chapter. We can, however, discuss broader trends through spelling evidence. The biggest difference between northern and southern consonants has historically been in **palatalisation**. I explained this briefly towards the beginning of the book, but palatalisation is a change that causes a consonant to be articulated closer to the palate than it was before the change. Before the various groups constituting the Anglo-Saxons migrated to Britain, a few of their dialects were affected by varying degrees of palatalisation in the velar plosives /k/ and /g/.

This made its way into most of the Old English dialects, as well as the Frisian languages to a lesser extent, and was governed by a number of rules. Proto Germanic /ɣ/ (which became /g/ in most other Germanic languages) and /k/ would become /j/ and /t͡ʃ/ respectively when followed by a front vowel. /ɣ/ was also affected after front vowels, unless it was followed by a back vowel. /k/ was only affected after /i/ and /i:/, unless it was followed by a back vowel. /sk/ clusters became /ʃ/ at the start of a word and after a front vowel - again, unless a back vowel followed. Finally, Proto-Germanic /ggj/ clusters became /dʒ/. This resulted in such modern words as *church, cheese, sheep, ship, bridge* and *ridge* in standard English.

In Cumbrian, there are numerous forms unaffected by palatalisation scattered throughout older texts and place names. Some examples are *kirk* ('church') /kʊrk/, *Keswick* (place name, equivalent of 'cheese-wick') /ˈkezɪk/, *brigg* ('bridge') /brɪg/ and *rigg* ('ridge') /rɪg/, among numerous others. All of these appear to be regular developments from the Old English forms *cirice, cēse, scēap, brycg* and *rycg*.

There are also forms cognate with English words that have been loaned in from Old Norse and thus do not show palatalisation, such as *kowp* ('to exchange'), *garn* ('yarn') and *garth* ('yard;

enclosure'). It's important not to jump on the idea of Scandinavian influence accounting for the lack of palatalisation in the affected native words. There is good reason to suspect that most West Germanic dialects immediately prior to the migration period did not show palatalisation, and the idea of one of those making its way to Britain and retaining its velar consonants is a more convincing explanation than that Scandniavian influence in the north caused already palatalised forms to re-velarise.

Many of these velar forms survived well into the 19th and 20th centuries, only to be overtaken by palatalised loan words from standard English. Middle English texts, including Chaucer's *Reeve's Tale*, have the velar form *ik* as the first-person singular pronoun in the north at that time (the form corresponding to the English word *I*).

Note that the presence of unpalatalised forms in later Cumbrian does not preclude the existence of palatalised forms in parts of Cumbria during the Anglo-Saxon period, but place name evidence suggests velar forms were widespread.

A curious but less-remarked-upon feature is the fronting of /ʃ/ to /s/. This is found throughout Middle English indentures from Cumbria in spellings such as *sal* ('shall') and *sud* ('should'), and some forms are recorded in the Orton survey, such as /ˈsʊgər/ for *sugar* and /ɐs/ for *ash*. However, the people giving these forms often commented that they were 'old' or likely to be used by one of their grandparents, meaning they were probably largely obsolete by, say, 1920. It is difficult to know whether these represent the elision of a velar /k/, or a fronting of an already-palatalised /ʃ/. Place name forms such as *skip* in *Skipton* suggest that /sk/ forms persisted in some places.

Old English /w/ has been retained as normal in most circumstances, so that *w* in later Cumbrian corresponds closely with /w/ in RP English. However, Old English *hw-* seems to have followed a different path. Those who have read a lot of northern Middle English texts will know that *qu-* is often used to spell words in the *what, when, where* lexical set, so that they are rendered *quat, quen, quere*. This is sometimes put down to a quirk of orthographic convention, and that the sound was /ʌ/ (a voiceless /w/) as it had been in Old English and continued to be in standard English until relatively recently. This sound has a range of exotic realisations in Scots dialects, including /f-/ and /kw-/. It could be argued (and I would argue) that a number of later Cumbrian forms point to a Middle English realisation of /kw-/ in parts of the north-west. *Wiet* ('quiet') /ˈwɐɪˌət/, *wick* ('alive') /wɪk/, *wishen* ('cushion') /ˈwɪʃən/. In *wheen-cat* ('female cat') in the *Glossarium Brigantinum*, the *wheen* appears to be cognate with standard English *queen*. I suspect that the *quick* consonant merged with the *what* consonant during the Middle English period, explaining *qu-* spellings, and that this process had finished by the time the *Glossarium* was compiled in the 1670s. In an analogous change, word-initial /θw-/ clusters reduced to /ʌʍ-/.

Old English /l/ has been retained everywhere, apart from in the conditions described in the section on long vowels. As already discussed, it's likely that during the 1600s, prior to the /ɐl/ > /ɐː/ > /ɔː/ change, there was a distinction between Cumbrian varieties that had velarised /ɫ/ between /ɐ/ and an alveolar plosive, and Cumbrian varieties who had 'clear' /l/ in all positions.

The nature of /r/ in Old English, particularly Northumbrian Old English, is debated. Roger Lass presents a good case that it was a uvular sound in some areas, such as [ʁ]. A similar sound survived well into the 20th century in the 'Northumbrian burr.' Later Cumbrian /r/ was realised as a tap [ɾ] or trill [r], and given its prevalence in world languages and in the rural dialects of Germanic languages, I tend to favour a system of free variation between these two for Cumbrian. I may re-think this view in a future publication, though.

The shift to non-rhoticity was in its early throes in 1913 when Brilioth was writing; /r/ was lost only between a stressed vowel and an alveolar plosive in coda position. As the 20th century progressed, this increased in scope. My grandfather, born in the mid 1930s, speaks almost entirely non-rhotically, only realising /r/ before a vowel most of the time. This is with the exception of what is called **intrusive 'r'**, a feature of a lot of non-rhotic British English dialects.

The intrusive 'r', for those unfamiliar, is the appearance of a rhotic between two words, where one word ends with a non-high vowel and the next starts with one. For example, in rapid speech, I would realise the phrase 'stamina up' as [ˈstamɪnəɹˈʌʔp], with an [ɹ] between the two words, even though neither word has historically contained a rhotic.

Occasionally, particularly when speaking to other Cumbrians, he will realise /r/ as an alveolar tap at the end of a word. Most young Cumbrians today have fully non-rhotic accents, pronouncing /r/ only before a vowel.

The Old English nasals /m/, /n/ and /ŋ/ appear to have been realised in the same way throughout the last millennium. However, when a nasal in the coda of a stressed syllable was followed by a voiced plosive in Old English, that voiced plosive has disappeared by later Cumbrian. Some resulting words are shown below:

RP	Cumbrian
Spindle /spɪndəl/	*Spinnel* /spɪnəl/
Finger /ˈfɪŋgə/	*Finger* /ˈfɪŋər/
Ember /ˈembə/	*Emmer* /ˈemər/
Bramble /ˈbɹæmbəl/	*Brimmel* /ˈbrɪməl/
Mumble /ˈmʌmbəl/	*Mummel* /ˈmʊməl/
Thimble /ˈθɪmbəl/	*Thimmel* /ˈθɪməl/
Longer /ˈlɒŋgə/	*Langer* /ˈleŋər/

This kind of change, and subsequent loaning into standard English, is likely to be the origin of words like *simmer*. This change is tricky to date; *spinnel* is found in Relph's poetry, putting the change before 1747. *Brimmel-kites* ('bramble berries') appears in the 1677 *Glossarium*. It is difficult to narrow down the date range in which the change may have happened any more than that.

Possibly alongside this change, we see loss of word-final /b/ after /m/, and loss of word-final /g/ after /ŋ/, in words like *lamb* [lɛm], *climb* [klɪm] or [tlɪm], *lang* [leŋ].

In Old English -*Vfen* clusters (where *V* represents any vowel), the /n/ has assimilated to the /f/ (realised as a [v] in Old English between two voiced sounds), and the unstressed vowel has disappeared. In later Cumbrian, these are found as [-Vbm̩] clusters, as in *ebm* ('even') [ˈebm̩], *sebm* ('seven') [ˈsebm̩], *yubm* ('oven') [ˈjʊbm̩]. Phonologically, it is probably simplest to represent /[- bm̩] as /-bən/ or /-bəm/.

/d/ in certain word-final environments can become /t/. Brilioth was unable to pinpoint the exact conditions that lead to this devoicing. I had a little poke around for an article for University of Melbourne linguistics society journal. The devoicing tends to happen in past simple forms - see *prentit* ('printed'), *weddit* ('wedded'), *gaddert* ('gathered'), but sound changes cannot have grammatical conditions, so there must be a deeper phonological explanation than this.

Word-final /d/ devoicing can be seen throughout north-western literature. Indentures made in Cumbria in the late Middle English period have -*t* as the standard ending for past simple forms extremely regularly. Brilioth remarks that where Old English word-final /d/ is in an unstressed syllable, or where it is in a consonant cluster, it usually becomes /t/, but that beyond that, the sound change 'follows no definite laws.' Examination of regional Middle English literature sheds some light on this; 15th-century indentures gathered from the University of Stavanger's Middle English Grammar Corpus (see further reading) show an extremely consistent change from original /-d/ to /-t/ when word-final and in an unstressed syllable. The reason it applies so commonly to preterites is because they often ended in *-Vd* in north-western Middle English, giving forms such as *payitt* ('paid'), *claymet* ('claimed'), *callet* ('called'). The fact that authors of the period seem to switch between <i> and <e> to spell this unstressed vowel, and the fact that many English dialects have a tendency to centralise unstressed vowels, points to a vowel quality something like [ɪ], so that a word like *payitt* would be pronounced /ˈpɛjɪt/. It's possible that this change caused people to view /-ɪt/ as the standard preterite ending, and to eventually over-apply it to preterites that would not have been affected by the sound change.

Old English intervocalic /d/ is retained in Cumbrian in some situations where it becomes a fricative in standard English:

RP	Cumbrian
Father /ˈfɑːðə/	*Fadder* /ˈfɐdər/
Leather /ˈleðə/	*Ledder* /ˈledər/
Feather /ˈfeðə/	*Fedder* /ˈfedər/
Bother /ˈbɒðə/	*Bodder* /ˈbɒdər/
Slither /ˈslɪðə/	*Sledder* /ˈsledər/
Nether /ˈneðə/	*Nedder* /ˈnedər/

By the late 19th century, and certainly by Brilioth's time, word-initial /kl-/ and /gl-/ clusters had become /tl-/ and /dl-/ in some variants of the dialect. The widespreadness of this is unclear, but it is not attested by Brilioth or by the Orton survey, suggesting disappearance or obselesence by about 1900.

In Old English, there seems to have been a complementary distribution between the phones [ç] and [x], both of which were allophones of the phoneme /h/. The phone [ç] was used in words like *siht* ('sight'), *niht* ('night') where the phoneme came after a front vowel. The phone [x] was used in words like *genōh* ('enough') and *rūh* ('rough') where the phoneme came after a back vowel. A very similar distribution exists in standard German today. In Cumbrian, as previously discussed, [ç] disappeared in words like *night* and *sight* between 1600 and 1800, and the vowel was lengthened to compensate. [x] has either disappeared altogether or become /f/, as in *slaghter* ('slaughter') [ˈslɐftər]. Because words in this lexical set were spelled with <gh> even after taking the found /f/, it is difficult to place when the change happened; it may have been in line with the disappearance of [ç], it may have been earlier. The fact that it is not remarked upon in 19th-century dialect literature (even by Dickinson, who comments on the disappearance of [ç]) suggests it was not later. In instances where [x] disappeared altogether, it may first have become labialised [xʷ], and then [ʍ], before finally voicing in words like *thought, nought*, producing the later forms *thowt* and *nowt*. Below is what I think is the most direct explanation of the development of *nought* in Cumbrian:

$$[nɒxt] \; > \; [nɒx^wt] \; > \; [nɒʌt] \; > \; [nɒʊt]$$

Aside from the cases given, all of the consonants seem to have followed broadly similar paths of development to their standard English counterparts.

The situation of the word *whol* ('hole') is unique. In later Cumbrian, and to this day in the speech of some Cumbrians, it is /wɔ:l/. However, its spelling (often beginning with <wh>) suggests that it must have been [ʍɔ:l] until some point in the 19th century, and this is in line with its expected phonological development from Middle English. The late Middle English pronunciation was /hɔ:l/. The fact that this, subject to the /ɔ: > wɔ:/ change, became [ʍɔ:l], suggests that [ʍ] in Cumbrian is the realisation of a phonological /hw/ cluster.

This harks back to the difference between **phones** and **phonemes** that I explained in the introduction to linguistics; the phoneme is the underlying concept of a sound within the mind of the speaker, and the phone is the way that this concept is realised when the speaker talks[7]. In this case, what the speaker considers to be a /hw-/ cluster (resulting in the change from /hɔ:l/ to /hwɔl/ and eventually to /hwɔ:l/) is actually realised as [ʍ] (the voiceless equivalent of [w]).

Of course, this is the same sound as we find at the beginning of more conservative pronunciations of *what* and *when* (and, in Cumbrian, *wheen* and *whick)* - the word *whol* falls into that same lexical set. When the [ʍ] in these words was voiced - or, to put it another way, when phonological /h/ was lost before /w/ - the word became /wɔ:l/.

---

[7] For any biologists reading, this is similar to the relationship between a genotype (the underlying genetic situation) and a phenotype (the realisation of those genes, which may differ from situation to situation and from organism to organism).

The development of the words *yam* ('home') and *yal* ('whole') can be visualised in a similar way. The late Middle English form of *yam* was /hɛːm/, which eventually became /hjɐm/, with the initial /hj-/ cluster probably being realised as [ç-] or [çj-]. Exactly when this cluster was reduced depends on which way we parse the phonology. If you remember, [ç] also existed in words like *neet* ('night') and *seet* ('sight') until relatively late-on, so the loss of phonetic [ç] at the beginning of /hjɐm/ might have been part of this change. Alternatively, it could be viewed as a loss of phonological /h/ before /j/.

Initial *kn-* clusters found in Old English seem to have been preserved in certain varieties of Cumbrian into the early 1800s as /tn-/, such as in *tnop* ('knob') and *tnit* ('knit'), as found in the poetry of Robert Anderson.

As promised, we now return to the finer details of consonant articulation. In later Cumbrian - at least, Cumbrian as recorded in the Orton survey - /t/ and /d/ are realised dentally when they occur before /ɾ/. Dental realisations of these plosives are by no means unheard-of in earlier English - John Hart, an advocate for spelling reform writing in the 1550s, describes what can only be dental /t/ and /d/ sounds in all positions. It may be that this was commonplace across English dialects before a certain point in time, or it may be that this is a development distinct from later Cumbrian dental realisations.

Affrication of certain plosives occurs in other north-western English varieties, notably that of Liverpool, and this has been attributed to Irish influence. The influx of Irish migrants to 19th-century Cumbria may therefore be taken as an explanation for this, and one which places a clear date before which the affrication cannot have happened - but it is equally possible that it is a Cumbrian innovation independent of external influence.

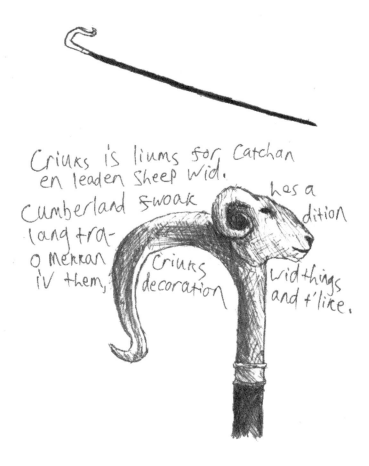

Criuks is liums for Catchan
en leaden sheep wid.
Cumberland swoak has a
lang tra-   dition
o mekkan
iv them,   Criuks
           decoration   widthings
                         and t'like.

Potential Scottish Origin of Long Vowels.

Over the last few chapters, I have taken the dialect of Cumbrian spoken in the 19th and 20th centuries and attempted to trace that dialect backwards through time. A modern understanding of historical linguistics makes this possible. However, this is to say little of the wider cultural situation of the dialect. Legal indentures from Cumbria in the 1400s, one of which is reproduced in the selected readings at the end of this book, resemble later Cumbrian in terms of vocabulary and spelling. However, aspects of the orthography of these documents, while not necessarily standing in opposition to my ideas about pre-vowel-shift Cumbrian, do not directly support them either.

To give an example: in the chapter on the long vowels, I argued that the vowel in the *home* lexical set was probably /ɛ:/ before the great vowel shift, on the basis of the comparative method and some sometimes-dismissed spelling evidence from Chaucer. In Cumbria, the vowel in this set is usually spelled with <a>. This spelling is actually consistent with some spellings from Agnes Wheeler's *Dialogues*, written in the late 1700s; *sake* is rendered as *saak*, and presumably would have been **sak* or **sake* in Cumbrian Middle English. If Wheeler's dialect represents a particularly conservative version of Cumbrian, the vowel quality in this lexical set may have been something like /ɐ:/ before, during and after the great vowel shift, at least in certain words. This may have been the case throughout most of Cumbria.

I still maintain that the modern forms are unlikely to have come from /ɐ:/, and are likely to be directly related to modern Scots pronunciations of *home* as /he:m/. If this is true, where was this /ɛ:/ realisation used, and where did it undergo the initial change to a centering diphthong?

My strong suspicion is that the bulk of the pre-vowel-shift changes in the long vowels occurred in southern Scotland, and that these values were picked up by Cumbrians, as well as people in other parts of northern England, at some point in the 1600s. I think that this idea works on a number of levels, and it is supported by philological evidence that actively works in its favour.

In historical linguistics, we often work by combining spelling evidence with what we know about common processes of sound change. However, we are occasionally treated to a text in which the author actually describes their own speech in a way that can be interpreted by modern linguists much less ambiguously than ordinary spelling evidence. Alexander Hume (no relation) is one such author. He describes his own Scottish pronunciation in *Of the Orthographie and Congruitie of the Britan Tongue*, probably written at some time between 1610 and 1620.

In his section *Of the Britan Vouales*, he establishes a few minimal pairs: pairs of words that are only distinguished by a difference in one phoneme (for example, *cat* and *bat*). I will go through this relatively short section here:

> *Of a, in our tongue we have four soundes, al so differing ane from an other, that they distinguish the verie signification of wordes, as, a tal man, a gud tal, a horse tal. Quherfoer in this case I wald commend to our men the imitation of the greek and latin, quho, to mend this crook, devysed diphthongs.*

Here, he mentions the words *tall, tale* (a story) and *tail* (of an animal). He uses the word 'diphthongs' where modern linguists would probably say 'digraphs'; pairs of letters, rather than pairs of sounds. We cannot necessarily assume that a digraph represents a diphthong, despite Hume's usage of the word. He goes on to describe the four sounds that are generally written with <a>, giving advice as to how he thinks they ought to be written in order to best represent the pronunciation he is accustomed to.

He says that the 'simplest' of the four sounds - that sound in *hal* ('hall') - should be written with <a> on its own. By 'simplest,' he presumably means the short monophthongal variant. This is probably /a/ or /ɐ/, which is in line with my suggestions in previous chapters. He then lists three minimal pairs of this word, which he spells *hael* ('a shower of hail'), *hail* ('hail Mary') and *heal* ('whole'). The last is particularly relevant, but I will examine the other two first.

Hael and *hail,* as he writes them, are nowadays both spelled *hail*. This is not reflective of their origins; the former ('a shower of hail') comes directly from the Old English word *hægl*, whereas the latter ('hail Mary') comes from the Old Norse loan word *heill*. To complicate things, the Old Norse *heill* is cognate with the English *whole*, which Hume lists as the fourth minimal pair. By spelling alone, I would give these values as 'a shower of /hɛ:l/', but '/haɪl/ Mary.' This is the reverse of what one might expect; after all, it presumes a sort of 'swapping' of vowel qualities between the two lexical sets, with OE /æj/ becoming /ɛ:/ and ON /ei/ becoming /aɪ/. This is explainable, albeit not in a straightforward way. I will give further detail on this later in the chapter.

The final lexical set is *heal* ('whole'). In Cumbrian, and indeed in Old English, this is the same as the *stone* lexical set. In the early 1600s, I would expect the ancestor to the later Cumbrian form to be something like /ɛə/. It is easy to see how <ea> could represent /ɛə/. It could conceivably also represent /ɛ:/, but this would require reanalysis of the first *hail* set. In interpreting the vowel in the *whole* set as /ɛə/, we find Hume's Scottish pronunciation to be a much better candidate for the ancestor of the later Cumbrian value.

I will temporarily skip ahead a few paragraphs to Hume's treatment of <o>. He says:

> *O, we sound al alyk. But of it we have sundrie diphthonges: oa, as to roar, a boar, a boat, a coat; oi, as coin, join, foil, soil; oo, as food, good, blood; ou, as house, mouse, &c.*

He seems to be saying that <o> has the same quality whether it stands alone or is part of a diphthong. This secondarily implies that the other vowels may differ in quality when pronounced as part of a diphthong. If we take this quality to be ancestral to modern Cumbrian forms, it could be anywhere between /ɒ/ and /o/, so I will assume it is /ɔ/ for the time being. The <oa> digraph he uses for *boat* and *coat* is best interpreted as a precursor to the sound in Cumbrian *bwoat, cwoat* - potentially /ɔə/ or something very similar. A viable alternative *would* be a long monophthong with a slightly different vowel quality - perhaps /ɒː/ - but Hume has already told us that <o> represents the same vowel quality wherever it appears. The vowel in the *book* set is, I think, best interpreted as long, probably monophthongal, /ɔː/. I would be tempted to suggest that the widespread Scottish quality at this time was /øː/, which is in line with later realisations, but it is possible that Hume is from an area where a pre-vowel-shift backed quality was retained. His spelling of *house* and *mouse* could be interpreted as in line with older southern (and more recent Scottish) pronunciations with /uː/, or they could be taken to be a narrow diphthong /ʊu/.

This introduces a possibility distinct from the one I suggest in the chapter on the long vowels; that the two roughly mid-height long vowels, /ɛː/ and /ɔː/, became centering diphthongs simultaneously, maintaining a high degree of symmetry throughout. The vowel in the *book* set is left to develop independently of this dynamic. Hume next addresses <e>:

> *Of e, we have tuae soundes, quhilk it is hard to judge quhilk is simplest; as, an el, ulna; and an el, anguilla; hel, infernus; and an hel, calx pedis. Heer I wald commend to our men quhae confoundes these the imitation of the south, quhilk doth wel distinguish these soundes, wryting the el, ulna, with the voual e, and eel, anguilla, with the diphthong ee. I am not ignorant that sum symbolizes this sound with a diphthong made of ie; eie, oculus; hiel, fiel, miel, etc. Here I am indifferent, and onelie wishes that the ane be used; let the advysed judge make choise of quhilk, for my awne paert I lyke the last best; 1. becaus eie, oculus, can not wel be symbolized ee; 2. because the greekes expresse η be εε, quhilk, as appeares be the Ioneanes and Doreanes, drawes neerar to α, than ε.*

He remarks that it is hard to judge whether the 'simplest' sound is the one in *el(bow)* and *hell*, or the one in *eel* and *heel*. To me, this implies that these two vowels share some feature that could be described as 'simple;' either shortness or monophthongality. Given all we know about these lexical sets elsewhere in English, the latter seems overwhelmingly more likely; they are both monophthongs, but the one in *eel* and *heel* is long.

He weighs up two common spellings of this sound, <ee> and <ie>. In his opinion, the latter is more representative of the sound in the *eel/heel* set. He gives two justifications for this. Firstly, he says [paraphrasing] "'eye' cannot be very well-captured by the spelling <ee>." This could be interpreted in more than one way. He could mean that the vowel quality in *eye* draws closer to /i/ than the spelling <ee> would have the reader believe. He could mean that the word *eye* consists of more than just one monophthong.

Secondly, he says [paraphrasing] 'the Greeks expressed Eta using εε which, going by evidence from the Ionians and Dorians, is nearer to α than ε.' In other words, <ee> is not a good spelling because it implies a lower vowel quality. Here, Hume gives us a strong hint that the value in *heel* is at the same height as, or higher than, the value in *hell*, which is what we would expect. The vowel in *heel* could be /eː/ or /iː/; the vowel in *hell* could be /ε/ or /e/.

> *Of i, also, our idiom receaves tuae soundes, as in a man's wil, and the wil of a fox. Heer, also, I wald have our men learne of the south, for these soundes they wel distinguish, wryting wil, fil, mil, stil, with i; and wyl, fyl, myl, styl, with y.*

Of <i>, Hume takes the pragmatic approach of accepting <i> for *will* and <y> for *wile*, telling us little about the vowel quality. However, he goes on to say (in a passage that I have not reproduced here because it is quite long) that he sees an 'eye of judgement' in some authors' decisions to spell the *wile* set with the Greek digraph <ει>, suggesting a diphthongal pronunciation of /ɛɪ/, /eɪ/ or /ɜɪ/, in line with southern pronunciations of this set at that time.

His lexical sets for the long vowels and diphthongs, as compared with those I have suggested for Cumbrian immediately after the vowel shift, are:

Hume	**Reconstruction**
Whole /hɛəl/	Whole /hɛəl/
Wile /wɛɪl/	Wile /wɛɪl/
Tale /tɛːl/	Tale /tɛːl/
Pail /paɪl/	Pail ???
Boat /bɔət/	Boat /bɔət/
Food /fɔːd ~ føːd/	Food /fiəd/
House /huːs ~ hɔʊs/	House /huːs/
Heel /heːl ~ hiːl/	Heel /hiːl/

These are far more consistent with one another than the values that might be taken from the spelling of Cumbrian indentures in the 1400s.

Dialect features can be projected outwards from centres of influence, especially if they are perceived as belonging to a high-prestige dialect. In southern England, while regional features persevere in all areas to some extent, clusters of features from the contemporary dialect of London have historically spread outwards. This accounts for noticeable phonological similarity between geographically separated historical dialects, such as those of Norfolk, the West Country and Hampshire. It has occurred recently enough that it can be heard in audio recordings; the prevalence of non-rhoticity in English has clearly spread outwards from London over the last century and a half. In several measureable ways, northern dialects have gradually become 'more southern' over the last century, with dialects more distant from London being less affected.

It makes perfect sense that the same 'beacon-of-influence' effect might have occurred in the early modern period around the

Scottish border. Bear in mind that this does not imply a dialect replacement, and nor is that implied by pre-vowel-shift texts - it only implies the adoption of certain aspects of early Scottish pronunciation. This needn't necessarily have been tied to any historical migration of people. The turbulent political situation in Scotland at the time could be brought in as a potential catalyst for such influence, but given that Cumbria is little more than 70 miles from Glasgow and Edinburgh, compared to more than 200 miles from London, a higher degree of Scottish influence is to be expected.

In that case, how did Cumbrian English sound in the decades leading up to the great vowel shift, before the Scottish developments of the long vowels were adopted? This is a bit more difficult to work out. For Scottish-influenced Cumbrian, we have sound recordings and living speakers who still use reflexes (modern versions) of the long vowels, which makes their historical counterparts easier to reconstruct. For the Cumbrian of the 1200s and 1300s, we do not have this. However, we do have spelling evidence from the 1400s, and spelling evidence from a variety of Cumbrian that seems to have retained some older features into the 1700s (see selected text IV at the end of the book).

As it happens, the differences don't look huge. In terms of 15th-century indentures (an excerpt from one of which can also be found in the selected readings), the all-important *stone* vowel is spelled with <a>, sometimes with <e> at the end of the word in a way that might indicate length; cf. *ane* ('one'), *dat* ('date'). Helpfully, Agnes Wheeler spells some words in this lexical set with <aa> in her dialogues from the 1700s; cf. *maar* ('more'), *saar* ('sore'), *saak* ('sake'), *waak* ('awake').

Based on this, it looks as though the vowel in this set had stayed very stable since the early Middle English period. The quality might have been anything from /aː/ to /ɐː/ to /ɑː/, and probably showed both diachronic and regional variation that we'll never know the detail of. By Wheeler's time, Scottish-influenced values are creeping into this set in some words; she spells *make* as *meeak*.

The other relevant set is the *book* set, which in 15th-century indentures is spelled, as today, with <oo>. This sound is always hard to interpret, as Scottish authors were almost certainly using it to spell fronted /ø:/ at the same time as southern authors were using it for /o:/ and subsequently /u:/. Agnes Wheeler spells this vowel <ea>, which I interpret as /i:/ for reasons outlined in the chapter on the long vowels. The Cumbrian vowel prior to the vowel shift could be anything from /o:/ to /ø:/ to /ɔ:/ to /œ:/ - none seems unreasonable to me. Having said all that, we might find this distribution in Cumbria itself, while accepting that some later Cumbrian vowel qualities are probably of non-Cumbrian origin:

Whole /hɐ:l/
Wile /wi:l/
Tale /tɐ:l/
Pail /pɐil/
Boat /bɔ:t/
Food /fo:d ~ fø:d/
House /hu:s/
Heel /he:l/

The dating of this is rather more complicated. Researchers such as Jeremy Smith, writing in 1994, remark that the vowel shift in the north seems to have been well underway by the time it started in the south; the early throes of it were perhaps already occurring in the 1200s, pushing our hanging chronology further back in time.
Wherever our hypothetical proto-Scottish-border dialect was spoken, a simple six-stage vowel shift could explain the changes I have suggested:

1. The vowels in *whole* /ɛ:/ and *boat* /ɔ:/ break to the centering diphthongs /ɛə/ and /ɔə/.

2. The vowel in *day* raises and smoothes to /ɛ:/ to fill the gap left by the vowel in *whole*.

3. The first element of the diphthong in *hail* lowers to /ai/ to fill the gap left by *day*.

4. The vowel in *time* breaks to /ei/ to fill the gap left by the vowel in the *hail* set.

5. The vowel in *heel* raises to /iː/ to fill the gap left by *time*.

6. Finally, possibly at a later stage, the vowel in *book* diphthongised to /iə/, possibly to address an assymetricality in the diphthong system: for example, to bring the number of centering diphthongs in line with the number of raising diphthongs. This will require further investigation.

Syntax & Sentence Constructions.

Any sufficiently divergent dialect of English will have aspects of grammar that differ from those of standard English, and Cumbrian is no exception. Most of the differences are to do with pronouns, verb conjugation and what kinds of sentence construction are considered natural and acceptable. Some of the greater points of divergence appear in 19th-century texts but are not noted in 20th-century analyses, suggesting that southern 'standard' grammar had started to erode away Cumbrian syntax by that time.

The first thing to note is that the copula works differently in later Cumbrian. The copula is the verb *to be*, and it is an extremely irregular verb in English, because it has numerous different forms depending on the context it appears in. If you're talking in the first person singular (that is, talking about just yourself) in standard English, you use the word *am*. In the second person singular, you use the word *are*. In the third person singular, you use the word *is*. In later Cumbrian, these forms are often all levelled to *is*.

> *Aa's nut owwer fain wid it.*
> I'm not very happy with it.
> (Lit. 'I is not over happy with it').

> *Thou's a laal yan, isn't the?*
> You're a little one, aren't you?
> (Lit. 'Thou is a little one, isn't thee?').

> *Some locals was commen en gaan...*
> Some locals were coming and going...
> (Lit. 'Some locals was coming and going...').

This is mentioned a few times in the Orton survey, and survives to this day in broader speakers. While this is one grammatical feature that is seen by some to mark one out as uneducated, there is nothing about this system that makes it less fit-for-purpose.

The pronoun still indicates who the speaker is talking about, so no ambiguity is created.

On the subject of pronouns, Cumbrian is one of several northern dialects that still makes a distinction between singular *thou* and plural *you*, albeit this is a marginal feature. While this is rare in younger speakers today (rarer, for example, than in Yorkshire), it was commonplace as little as fifty years ago, and was almost certainly universal[8] in the 19th century. It's likely that a distinction between *thou* (nominative) and *thee* (accusative) was retained until fairly late-on, but this is difficult to know for certain, because it was very often unstressed, meaning *thou* and *thee* were both rendered as /ðə/, spelled *the* in most texts. I am only aware of *thou* being in use today, so it's possible that the distinction has been levelled in speakers who still use this pronoun.

> *The's come heear nin mair!*
> You'll never come back here!
> (Lit. 'Thou-shall come here none more!').

> *Did she seem off til the?*
> Did she seem off to you?

For those less familiar with grammatical terms, nouns in English usually take either the **nominative** or the **accusative** case. The nominative case is applied when the noun is the **subject** of a sentence: that is, the noun is performing an action. The accusative case is applied when the noun is the **object**; the action is being done to it. English pronouns may change their form depending on whether they take the nominative or accusative case. Overleaf is a table to illustrate how this works, and where *thou* and *thee* fit into it.

---

[8] That is, understood and naturally used by almost all native speakers of the dialect. It is probable that in certain social situations, 'you' was applied to everybody.

Nominative	Accusative
I	Me
We	Us
He	Him
She	Her
It	It
Thou	Thee

The **reflexive** forms of pronouns also take unusual forms in Cumbrian. These are shown below:

St. English	Cumbrian
Myself	Misel /mɪˈsel/
Yourself	Yersel /jərˈsel/
Thyself	Thissel /ðɪˈsel/
Himself	Hissel /hɪ(z)ˈsel/
Herself	Hersel /hərˈsel/
Themselves	Theirsels /ðərˈselz/
Ourselves	Oorsels /ˌuːərˈselz/

These are in contrast to north-eastern forms ending in -*sen*, a reduction of the Middle English form *selven* ('self').
These forms of the reflexive -*self* are very old. Middle English texts from the area that is now Cumbria show both -*self* and -*sel* forms during the 1400s; one early example of -*sel* can be found in a 1441 agreement made near Eaglesfield.

> *In wytnes of þe whylk ath and concord þe saides*
> *elizabeth and John þe son to þis wrytyng has set to þair*
> *sellys.*
> 'In witness of which oath and concord the said Elizabeth and John the son to this writing has set to themselves.'

The form found here is *þair sellys* for what would later be *theirsels*. I should point out that in Middle English, the plural marker is often written as -*es* or -*ys* rather than just -*s*, so this spelling is not out-of-the-ordinary.

To **conjugate** a verb is to change the form of that verb depending on its context. In English, we conjugate verbs based on the nominative pronoun that comes before them. For example, you would say *I go*, but *he goes*; when you're talking about *he*, you have to add an extra part to the end of the verb *go*. Broad northern English dialects have always conjugated verbs slightly differently to standard English. Here is a graph of verb endings in later Cumbrian, applied to the word *hear*:

I hear	*We hear / hears*
Thou hears	*You hear / hears*
He/she/it hears	*They hear / hears*

This can vary from region to region and from person to person, but this is the system at its most divergent from standard English. Here is the system of verb endings found in the manuscript *Sir Gawain & the Green Knight* from the north-west midlands, just south of Cumbria, in the 1300s, applied to the same word:

I here	*We heres / heren*
Þou heres	*You heres / heren*
He/she/it heres	*Þay heres / heren*

A very similar pattern of conjugation is found. Again, this is no less fit-for-purpose than the standard English system, and is not a source of any ambiguity in the dialect. It has arisen naturally, just as the standard English system has, and it is perfectly functional to speakers who use it.

As I touched upon at the beginning of this chapter, the conjugation of the copula is levelled in broad later Cumbrian;

> *Aa's gaan til t'market.*
> I'm going to the market.
> (Lit. 'I is going to the market.')

> *Aa were liuken efter't.*
> I was looking after it.
> (Lit. 'I were looking after it.')

Cumbrian speakers will often use *them* as a determiner, where standard English would have *those*. For example, *those houses* would be *them houses*. This is not uniquely Cumbrian, but is widespread in English today, although it is considered by many to be incorrect. The word *them* comes from Old Norse, in which it could be used as a determiner; in northern dialects, it is likely that this emerged instead of the Old-English-derived form *those*.

> *Git them eggs i t'basket.*
> Get those eggs in the basket.

Nouns relating to time generally take no plural marker in later Cumbrian: *three years* becomes *three year*, *nine weeks* becomes *nine week*. This is common in older speakers today.
Being as some unique prepositions survive in the Cumbrian dialect to this day, I will start by explaining them. Most of the more common unusual prepositions are of Old Norse origin. Some are now gone altogether, but some are used by older speakers in the 2020s. I will speak about them all in the present tense for ease of reading, but bear in mind many are now archaic.
Later Cumbrian retains a distinction between *et* and *til* that existed in Old Norse, and is also retained by modern north Germanic languages. In English, both words can be translated to *to*, but there is an important difference in usage between them. *At* or *et* is used as the marker of the infinitive. Some examples of this, with English translations, are as follows:

> *Aa léuv et gang uutseyde.*
> I love to go outside.

> *It's hard et weel amell yan en t'ither.*
> It's hard to choose between one and the other.

This is directly analogous (and cognate) to Icelandic *að*, Norwegian *å* and Swedish *att*. On the other hand, most other senses of the English word *to* are covered by Cumbrian *til*, which also exists in the modern Scandinavian languages.

> *Aa's gang til Keswick et find a sheep.*
> I will go to Keswick to find a sheep.

> *Aa said't til him fower teymes.*
> I said it to him four times.

> *It matters laal til me.*
> It matters little to me.

Several Scots dialects also borrowed *til* from Old Norse, although many use *tae*, related to the English *to*. Older dialect literature will often have it as *tull*, which may well represent the weak form /təl/ or just /tl/. The distinction between *et* and *til* is very consistent in later Cumbrian.

Cumbrian has also carried forward a trend used in both Old Norse and Old English whereby certain words are prefixed with *a-* (*á* in Old Norse, *ā* in Old English). The habit of forming prepositions in this way is more likely to be due to Old Norse influence, because *á* was a preposition in its own right, roughly equivalent to English *on*. In fact, the word *aback* is often analysed as coming from Old English *on bæc*. I disagree; I think it comes from unattested Old Norse *á bak, which has exactly the same meaning if broken down to its constituent parts.

I think this for a couple of reasons; firstly, Cumbrian has so many more core-vocabulary Old Norse-derived words than standard English (even ignoring those with questionable etymologies). Secondly, the Old English origin would require the elision of /n/, while the Old Norse origin would not. It isn't overwhelming evidence, but on balance, the Old Norse origin seems more likely to me in this instance.

Aback is often used in conjuction with *on*, as in *aback on* ('behind'). *On* is often used by Cumbrians in the same situations as standard English would have *of*, so this is tantamount to *on back of*[9].

If *aback* is of Old Norse origin, what about another Cumbrian preposition of the same meaning, *ahint* (behind)? A regular sound change in later Cumbrian turns word-final /d/ into /t/, so *hint* is presumably related to the *-hind* part of *behind*. The Old English cognate here is *hindan*, whereas the Old Norse cognate is *handan*. There is no regular sound change that would explain the evolution of *hand(an)* into *hint*, but it's exactly the outcome you would expect from *hindan*. This may be evidence of the Old Norse preposition *á* being used productively by people who were also using the Old English word *hindan*. This could be a clue either that *á* (on) was at least briefly used in northern Old English as a loan word, or that there was a certain level of bilingualism to the point that people felt comfortable mixing vocabulary in their own speech. It's also possible that it came about as later speakers calqued the *a-* prefix onto other words. *Amell* (between) probably reflects Old Norse *á milli*, which is widely attested. *Anent* (on top of) is a bit of a messy one; it is usually given as somehow coming from Proto Germanic **ana ebnaz*, where **ebnaz* is cognate with English *even*; the original implication was probably 'on a level/even surface.' This is likely to have come via Old English rather than Old Norse, because **ebnaz* gives Old Norse *jafn*, from which there is no clear path of sound change to *-ent*. Old English has it as *efen*, which in some cases is reduced to *emn*.

The word *onemn* is actually attested in Old English, with a

---

[9] Whenever I talk about prepositions in one language being 'equivalent to' prepositions in another, remember that this is slightly reductive. Prepositions are abstract and can be used in a range of situations, and they prepositions in one language very rarely map perfectly onto those in another, although there is often overlap. They are not defined by any tangible thing in the world, but by the situations they are used in. To some extent this is true of all words, but it is very obvious with prepositions.

meaning more like 'nearby.' I can only imagine that a related word existed in Northumbrian Old English - something vaguely resembling *onemned - with the meaning 'on top of (a level surface)', and this was reduced to something like /ɔnˈend/, /ənˈend/ (depending on how vowels in unstressed syllables were treated at the time). The word-final /d/ - /t/ change gave /ənˈent/. Not knowing the etymology, later writers may have analysed this as being a-nent by analogy with a-back, a-mell, rather than the more etymological on-ent. The unstressed first vowel at that stage would have been reduced to /ə/, obscuring its original quality completely.

Aboon (above) must come from Old English *abufan*, but whereas in standard English the -an ending has disappeared, it has been preserved in Cumbrian, and the consonant [v] (an allophone of /f/) deleted, with the /u/ undergoing compensatory lengthening.

Iv is difficult to translate. It is cognate with English of (probably from *æf*, a nonstandard Old English variant), but it does not always correspond semantically with the modern English word. In the poem *Kéaty Curbison Cat*, the cat is said at one point to be *tiet iv a meelbag* (tied in a meal-bag). In the prose piece *Joe and the Geologist*, the father remarks that he doesn't want to go raking over the fells *iv a fine day like this*. It could probably be used largely interchangeably with *on* and *in*. As previously stated, the meaning of *on* is used in the same way as *of* is used in English; *aa's nivver hard on't* (I've never heard of it). Either the meanings of the two words have been levelled, or the different words were popular in different regions.

Here are a few illustrative sentences of the prepositions discussed here;

> *T'mus yud intil t'wohl i t'wo. T'rebm sat anent't.*
> The mouse ran into the hole in the wall. The raven sat on top of it.

> *Jwosep sat i t'sattle. Hetty sat iv t'flooer.*
> Jwosep sat in the chair. Hetty sat on the floor.

T'gaut lowpt owwer t'yat, t'frosk lowpt anonder't.
The boar jumped over the gate, the frog jumped under it.

T'frow were agéat. T'horse were aback on her.
The woman was on the road. The horse was behind her.

The definite article, as in many northern dialects, is /t/. The exact nature of it is debatable; most 19th-century writers, and most modern writers who use it, have analysed it as being a part of the word it applies to, so that *the horse* would become *t'horse*. Occasionally, it is analysed as being attached to the previous word; *from the horse's mouth* could be written *frae't horse muuth.* Note the lack of possessive *-s* at the end of *horse.* In any case, older writers (and my own experience with modern speakers) indicate that there is generally no vowel between the definite article and the word it applies to; not even /ə/. In later Yorkshire accents, the same definite article has sometimes been reduced to a glottal stop; this is not the case in older Cumbrian speakers' accents today, and none of the literature I have read from previous centuries mentions it then, either. This means that some very awkward consonant clusters are permitted in later Cumbrian, which were probably pronounced fully in most cases (no matter how tricky the reader may find it to pronounce them). For example, *t'gréavven man* (the digging man) would be pronounced /tgɾˈjɐvən mɛn/.

The development of this definite article has been much speculated upon; my initial view of it came from a 19th-century book, but I'm afraid I don't remember which one. That was that the Old English neuter definite article *þæt* had been clipped to its final sound, /t/. This made sense to me because I thought it was unlikely that the word *the* could be reduced to /t/, having no /t/ sound in it. However, elsewhere in Cumbrian, we find forms where this has clearly happened. Second-person singular verb forms can be suffixed with *-ta* (presumably pronounced weak, as /tə/) to form a question.

Kensta *whoar he's got til?*
Do you know where he's got to?
(Lit.) **Knows-thou** where he's got to?

In that case, it's easy to imagine *the* becoming *t*. Relph's poetry also has the form *th'* attested from the 1740s, suggesting an intermediate stage. He uses it interchangeably with *t*. Likewise, Agnes Wheeler, at the end of her collection of dialogues and fragments in the Westmorland dialect, gives both *th* and *t*, treating both as a suffix to the previous word.

Modern realisations of the article as a glottal stop, which only occurs word-finally, mean that it is probably best analysed as being attached to the previous word. Using the example *duun't pub* ('down the pub'), this could be analysed as the word *pub* being definite, and the word *duun* being changed to agree with the definiteness of *pub*.

This leads neatly onto a syntactic point. It seems to have been permissible, in later Cumbrian, to use sentence constructions without do-support.

> *Wits Jwoan whoar my spinnel is?*
> Does Jwoan know where my spindle is?
> (Lit.) Knows Jwoan where my spindle is?

This is used for comedic effect in the story *Bobby Banks Bodderment*, a genuinely funny little tale that I will examine later in this book;

> *Says Betty, says she, says Betty til me…*
> [Then] Betty says, [then] she says, [then] Betty says to me…

This is reminiscent of older standard English constructions before do-support became so widespread, for example *hast thou…?* rather than *do you have…?*

As I touched on a couple of pages ago, the deletion of the

possessive -*s* is well-attested in Cumbrian. This applies across-the-board in dialects and idiolects where it is found;

> *T'cuu muuth fell oppen, en it girse fell uut.*
> The cow's mouth fell open, and it's grass fell out.

> *Limpen, trailen't ahint it wid t'string ruund it neck…*
> Limping, trailing it behind it with the string round its neck…

Other common constructions are best given through examples. Note that I use idiomatic translations because although the literal translations may work in standard English, they do not necessarily convey the meaning very well.

> *Aa waddent cud gang, gif aa hedn't legs.*
> I wouldn't be able to walk if I didn't have legs.
> (Lit. 'I wouldn't could go, if I hadn't legs.')

> *He waddent cud see't past t'wo.*
> He wouldn't be able to see it past the wall.
> (N.b. 'wouldn't could' is still used in Cumbria)

> *Git away wid it! He nivver said that!*
> Come off it! He can't have said that!

> *Is Carel tuun ho' still stannen yet?*[10]
> Is Carlisle town hall still standing?

> *Diun't let's get sad owwer't.*
> Let's not get sad about it.

> *'Iv it ee, we med say, for it nobbut hed yan.'*
> Of its eye, we might say, for it only had one.

---

[10] *Yet* retains its older sense of 'still.'

He nobbut hed hard clay and stéans.
He only had hard clay and stones.

Aa's mair et déu, nor et ga léukan for a muus i a bower!
I've more to do than go looking for a mouse in a parlour!

I theear, we keep oor starkest sarks.
In there, we keep our stiffest shirts.

We's gang til t'market Setterda neest!
We will go to the market next Saturday!

Mey fworgangers nivver hed fud sek leyke this.
My ancestors never had food like this.

Aa's nivver ligt mey een on sek a thing as that.
I've never lain my eyes on anything like that.

Ya day, we sall o' lig low en stark.
One day, we will all lie low and still.

Aa killt a Brock; it's liggen low.
I killed a badger; it's dead.
(N.b. to *lig low* ('lie low') was a common euphemism for being dead).

Od skerse! Rotten thing nar on brayt ma.
Bloody hell! Stupid thing nearly hit me.

We were nar on Kezik when we saw't.
We were near Keswick when we saw it.

Aa's seen us gang til Coadbek iv a Sunda.
It's not unheard of for me to go to Caldbeck on a Sunday.

(N.b. *aa's seen us/I've seen us* is sometimes used to
mean 'it is not unheard of for me to…').

Aa lafft - aa were i Branthet t'ither day…
I laughed - I was in Branthet the other day…
(N.b. *aa lafft* ('I laughed') is sometimes used to
introduce a funny anecdote).

Discourse markers such as *like* and *you know* are often planted at
the ends of sentences in the Orton survey recordings:

It's nut a big dog, leyke.
It's not a big dog.

The extra meaning this discourse marker adds to a sentence is
difficult to qualify. It is only ever affixed to statements, never
questions. If I were to try to explain it from my own experience
of relatives using it, I would say that has a similar function to
saying *incidentally* or *by the way* in standard English, signalling
that the information preceding it is additional, and not vital to the
point being made. I don't think it's used in the same way by older
Cumbrian speakers as it is by, for example, younger north-
eastern speakers, who I have heard use it more generally. That's
all anecdotal, and should be taken with a pinch of salt.
Some scenarios that require a relative pronoun in standard
English do not require one in Cumbrian - the Orton survey notes
the sentence *there was a swarm of bees come over*, rather than *a
swarm of bees came over* or *there was a swarm of bees that
came over*. Likewise, *there was two children come*, rather than
there were two children that came.
In other northern dialects, a verb phrase can be inverted in
particular circumstances:

He med gud shun, did this fella.
This fella made good shoes.
(Lit. 'He made good shoes, did this fella.')

They've langer legs, hev horses.
Horses have longer legs.

They kill a gud mowdywarp, at diu them men.
Those men are good at killing moles.
(Lit. 'They kill a good mole, that do them men.')

Cumbrian has a slightly wider variety of irregular plural forms, some of which accord to Germanic i-mutation patterns found in pairs like *mouse-mice* in standard English, some of which do not:

Ee ('eye') /iː/	*Een* ('eyes') /iːn/
Shoe /ʃɪə/	*Shun* ('shoes') /ʃʊn/
Cu ('cow') /kuː/	*Kye* ('cows') /kɐɪ/

The first and last are regular survivals of the Old English plurals *ēagen* and *cȳ*.
We mustn't forget that by the 19th century, some southern influence will already have worn away aspects of northern pronunciation and vocabulary. A handful of unique forms exist in northern Middle English that do not reach later Cumbrian. One of these is the form *ik* ('I'), the unpalatalised form of southern Middle English *ich*. Chaucer makes use of this in *The Reeve's Tale*, although it is not specified from where in the north those characters come. The ending *-and*, rather than *-ing*, seems to have been commonplace for the present participle well into the Middle English period, so *singing* would be *singand*, *walking* would be *walkand* etc. The later Cumbrian present participle form tends to be /ən/, which could realistically be a reduction of both *-and* and *-ing*; which form survives into later Cumbrian is something of a moot point.
One thing the literature hints at is a certain pluralism in naming conventions. When one looks at censuses, one finds the sorts of names one would expect of England in the 19th century; Joseph, Christopher, John, Mary, Martha, Beatrice and so on. However, in dialect literature, you very rarely see names given in this way;

they are given in a form more consistent with Cumbrian phonology. You find *Jwohn* /d͡ʒwɔːn/ for 'John,' *Wutty* /'wʊtɪ/ for 'Walter,' *Keate* /kjɐt/ for 'Katherine' and so on. In what circumstances people would have been referred to by their census names is difficult to say.

While these 'Cumbrianised' names certainly existed, and persisted into the 20th century, I would like to know whether they were viewed in the same way as nicknames are viewed nowadays - that is, nobody considers it to be the person's 'actual' name, but it is the most commonly used one among peers - or whether the Cumbrianised name was considered to be the person's actual name.

Ya oad word for a sheep
was 'sowd', frae Old Norse
'sauðr'.

Earlier Writers' Observations.

Börje Brilioth, the Swedish author of *A Grammar of the Dialect of Lorton*, treats Cumbrian in terms of both pronunciation and syntax as though it is a foreign language. He does not solely focus on its differences from standard English, as I have done; he builds it up from the ground. He does, however, include lists of irregular plurals, as I did in the last chapter, noting that plural forms ending in *-s* are sometimes doubled, especially in the case of numerals: *twos* becomes *twoses*, *threes* becomes *threeses*. This appears in the Orton dialect survey 40 years later, noting *elevenses*, a meal eaten at eleven o'clock in the morning. Brilioth mentions that words expressing measurements are often not modified in the plural, which continues to be the case in modern Cumbrian. *Three pund* ('three pounds'), *sebm uunce* ('seven ounces').

He describes the **genitive**[11] case as being similar to in standard English, but occasionally having its ending doubled, as with plurals (so *John's apple* may be *Jwohn'ses apple*). However, he also remarks upon the omission of the possessive ending altogether by some speakers, as I have said.

Brilioth then makes a remark that I have thus far avoided making, because I have not been sure how to word it in an academic way. He says this:

> *'One of the most striking mannerisms of the true Cumbrian dialect-speaker is his tendency to avoid - as far as possible - making a definite statement of any kind.'*

This is something I had noticed in modern broad speakers and in 19th-century literature. The bush is thoroughly beaten-about. For an example, look to the chapter on phonology. The Orton quote from Albert Davidson; rather than saying *he was a fussy*

---

[11] The genitive is the grammatical case indicating possession or association, and is marginal in a lot of aspects of English speech. It might be better called the 'possessive.'

old schoolmaster, he opts to say *he was rather a fussy old sort of a schoolmaster*. Statements are very often framed in this way in Cumbrian, and it reflects a deeper attitude of general indifference to what one is saying. Even if this attitude is not held, it must be implied by the speaker. In particular, insults, the ends of anecdotes and the punchlines of jokes are worded in a very non-committal or roundabout way.

The suffix *-like* can be added to an adjective to lessen its effect, in the same way as *-ish* can in both standard English and Cumbrian. For example, *ruundlike* ('roundish'), *daftlike* ('a bit daft'). This seems to have been **productive**[12] in later Cumbrian. This is probably a continuity of the Old English suffix *-līc*, and cognate with the German *-lich*, used in the same way. You could come up with numerous cognate pairs between German and Cumbrian that feature this suffix; *dichlich* ('a bit fat') and *thicklike* ('thickish'), *befremdlich* ('strange') and *fremdlike* ('strange-ish'), and so on.

Brilioth further notes that two adjectives meaning the same thing are often paired up for emphasis; *t'ancient auld man* ('the ancient old man'), *a laal little thing* ('a little little thing'). Alternatively, as in English, an intensifying adverb can be added to the clause. He uses the example of *gae* /gɛː/: *a gay bonnie lass* ('a very pretty girl'). I would add *sair* ('sore; very'), which was originally an adjective used as an adverb, but in later Cumbrian seems to have evolved into an intensifying adverb: *it's sair cald uut theear* ('it's very cold out there'). The German cognate, *sehr*, can be used in exactly the same way: *es ist sehr kalt da draußen* ('it's very cold out there').

Comparatives are formed in the same way as in English, but more regularly with *-er* and *-est* where English would have *more* and *most* in some situations. For example, rather than saying

---

[12] If a prefix or suffix is 'productive,' that means that it can still be added to words to create new words. For example, *-ish* is a productive suffix in English, because you can add it to more-or-less any adjective and make a new word, and people will know what you mean.

more comfortable and *most comfortable*, a later Cumbrian speaker would say *comfortabler* and *comfortablest*. This is with the exception of seven words listed by Brilioth, only a couple of which differ from standard English. These are *bad*, whose forms are *war* /wɐːr/[13] and *warst* /wɐːrst/; *laal* ('small'), /ˈlɐːlər/ and /liːst/; *lyat* ('late') whose superlative is *last*[14].

He also lists *nar* [nɐːr] ('near'), whose forms he gives as *narer* and *nekst*. I would add that an older Cumbrian form of *next* is *neest*; this makes sense when one considers the origin of *next* in standard English.

Near and *next* were once the comparitive and superlative forms of *nigh* ('close'). In other words, rather than having *nigh, nigher, nighest*, you had *nigh, near, next*. This distribution has obviously been broken up in English today, and few people realise that the words are related to each other now. The Middle English form of *nigh* was pronounced [niç], which in Cumbrian lost its final consonant and lengthened the vowel at some point after the great vowel shift, giving /niː/. This is the form we find in later Cumbrian, spelled *nee*. The superlative followed a regular development along the same lines; /niçst/ lost its medial consonant and the vowel underwent compensatory lengthening, giving /niːst/. This is the exact same process as gave rise to *neet* ('night'), *reet* ('right') and *hee* ('high'); see the chapter on long vowels for further explanation.

The comparative and superlative can also be formed by adding -*mer* /mər/ or -*mest* /məst/ to the ends of adjectives, analogous to the process that formed English *former* and *foremost*. This is applied more widely in Cumbrian; Brilioth gives *low* /lɔː/, *lowmer* /ˈlɔːmər/, *lowmost* /ˈlɔːməst/.

Brilioth then describes the forms of numbers, which I will

---

[13] Brilioth remarks that this form probably comes from Old Norse *verr*, which at the time of its loaning into northern English would have been pronounced with initial /w/.

[14] English 'last' is actually a syncopated form of 'latest', but most of us no longer view it as the superlative of 'late,' but as a word in its own right.

include here because they have already been written about in a
lot of detail in other books. I will go up to twelve because
English has twelve unique numbers before elements start to
repeat themselves.

Yan /jɐn/	*Sebm* /ˈsebən/
Twee /twɪə/	*Eight* /ɛːt/
Three /θriː/	*Nine* /nɐɪn/
Fower /ˈfɐʊwər/	*Ten* /ten/
Five /fɐɪv/	*Lebm* /ˈlebən/
Six /sɪks/	*Twelve* /twelv/

Numerals such as *twenty-one, thirty-six, fifty-eight* etc. are
formed in the same way as they are in English when counting,
but otherwise follow the pattern *yan-en-twenty* ('one-and-
twenty'), *six-en-thirty* ('six-and-thirty') etc. Ordinal forms (the
equivalents of English *first, second, third* etc.) are formed with -
t; *fift, sixt, sebmt* etc., aside from the first three which are
irregular, as in standard English; *fust* /fʊrst/ ('first'), *second*
/ˈsekənd/, *third* /ˈθʊːrd/.

It's here that I will mention one of the much-discussed and
much-advertised oddities of the Cumbrian dialect: the sheep-
counting system comprising the numbers *yan, tyan, tethera,
methera* etc. I must admit I am not very familiar with it, on the
one hand because my family does not use it and on the other
hand because it rarely appears in old dialect literature, which
leads me to wonder whether it may be a recent borrowing from a
nearby dialect area. The form of the numbers is slightly different
from place to place, but show descent from a Celtic language
related to Welsh, albeit with significant alteration over the years
so that several pairs of numbers rhyme.

The only number clearly of Old English descent is *yan*, which is
the regular development from OE *ān* that we would expect in
Cumbrian.

The counting system is supposed to be used for counting sheep
or for knitting, and is rarely-used outside of these and similar
contexts in ordinary speech, with the normal reflexes of Old

English numerals being used most of the time. I would be hard-pushed to give any constructive comment on the origin of this system, other than it may have been borrowed from a Celtic language when they were last widespread, fostered in a particular dialect or series of dialects where it rearranged itself into the rhyming system that now exists, and was perhaps lent back into Cumbrian at a later time. It's possible that *yan, tyan, tethera* has existed in Cumbria for a long time, but I can't say so with any confidence: the regular OE-derived forms are the only numbers ever attested in writing from the 19th century, so it is possible that the system didn't exist (or at least wasn't common) in Cumbria at that time. I think it might have been a recent introduction, although it's possible that I am completely wrong, and that the dialectographers were just looking in the wrong areas. In any case, it is well-established in Cumbrian popular memory now.

Brilioth covers the pronouns from an etymological viewpoint, suggesting that *you* /juː/ is a post-vowel-shift loan from standard English, given that the surrounding dialects use *ye* /jiː/ in its place. The expected native Cumbrian form of the word would be something like *yow* /jɛʊ/, which would be a homophone with *yow* ('ewe'). In some Cumbrian varieties in use at his time, there was still a distinction between the nominative *thou* and the accusative *thee* that I describe in the chapter on usage and syntax.

There is another preserved distinction, as well: a common distinction in European languages which standard English lacks, called the T-V or 'tu-vos' distinction[15]. This distinction only exists in the second-person singular. It meant that you would use *thou* to address people like friends, peers and your children, whereas *you* would be used to address superiors, your employer, your parents and people of a higher class than you. You also might use it to address somebody you'd just met, to avoid offending them. However, as I say, this distinction was only

---

[15] It's called this because in Latin, it affected the second-person pronouns *tu* and *vos*.

made in the singular; the plural pronoun was always *you*.

	Singular	Plural
Nominative	Thou *(to friends, peers, people of lower status)*	You
	You *(to parents, your employer, people of higher status)*	You
Accusative	Thee *(to friends, peers, people of lower status)*	You
	You *(to parents, your employer, people of higher status)*	You

Finally, Brilioth goes through the ways in which the **past simple** is formed in Cumbrian strong verbs. Rather than reproducing the full table, I will give a few examples. Strong verbs with the vowel /ɐɪ/ form the past simple with the /jɐ/ sequence. *Bide* /ɐɪ/ becomes *byad* ('bode') /bjɐd/; *write* /rɐɪt/ becomes *wryat* ('wrote') /rjɐt/. Such forms seem to have become rare by the mid 20th-century.

A wealth of further information about verb conjugation can be found in *A Grammar of the Lorton Dialect* by Börje Brilioth, which can (at the time of writing) be found online with a quick search. I will not reproduce it all here because there would be little value in it, and I can offer no useful amendment to it.

The next piece of literature to which I will turn my attention is the 1905 *Supplement to the Glossary of the Dialect of Cumberland* by E. Prevost and S. Dickson-Brown, which highlights a number of other interesting syntactic features. Dickson-Brown describes the distribution of words for 'no.' The form *nay* /nɛː/ is used when the speaker disagrees with something that has been said. This is the expected reflex from Old Norse *nei*. On the other hand, the word *neah* /niː, nɪə/ is an **assent to the negative** - that is, it's an agreement with a negative statement that has been made. For example, in this exchange:

> John: *"T'wedder's nut been gud iv late."*
> Jill: *"Neah, it's nut."*

Jill says *neah* because John has made a negative statement, and she agrees with it. The form /niː/ is a regular development from Old English *nē*; the form /nɪə/ from *ā*. Alternatively, *no* /nɔː/ is a categorical, strong 'no.' This is probably a late borrowing from standard English; the only way it could have arisen as a native Cumbrian word are from an original Middle English **nall* (which is not attested). If it was loan into north-western English during the Middle English period, it would give the form /nwɔː/, which is not as Dickson-Brown describes it.

His opinion of the prepositions is that several of them have become phonologically reduced to the point of being interchangeable, as they are so often just /ə/ in rapid speech. While I would agree that reduction may have levelled them in writing, as authors (particularly non-native speakers of Cumbrian) will often mix up the letters they use to represent them, I think that an underlying distinction between the prepositions was probably maintained into later Cumbrian. As I touched upon in the chapter on syntax, prepositions are difficult words to define; they do not have definitions so much as applications. Try to list all the different ways the word *in* is used in standard English, and you will probably have trouble. The disparity in usage between later Cumbrian prepositions and English ones is great enough that it can be easy to look at them and see no pattern, but I maintain that there probably is one, albeit one that might have been different from place to place. The lack of a pattern is an illusion amplified by the idea that prepositions will map consistently onto each other between different language varieties, whereas in fact they often do not overlap a huge amount.

The next thing the author highlights is noun phrases composed of a preposition followed by a verb. He gives the examples *doonfo'* /ˈduːnfɔː/ ('downfall'), *uptak* /ˈʊptɛk/, *intak* /ˈɪntɛk/

('intake'), *offcum* /ˈɒfkʊm/ ('offcome'), *ootgang* /ˈuːtgɐŋ/ ('out-go; way out, exit'). These bear a striking resemblance to German separable-prefix verbs[16], but work in a different way because they are nouns. *Ootgang* is cognate with German *Ausgang* ('way out, exit').

The word *hooiver* ('however') can be affixed to the end of a sentence or anecdote to indicate that the speaker has finished speaking. I would add that this can be done in standard English with the word *anyway*.

The author makes a few comments agreeing with Brilioth's, that Cumbrian sentence constructions are often unnecessarily round-about, as though there is some cultural value in finding creative ways of not quite saying things. Instead of *varra seun* ('very soon'), you would often hear *afwore it be varra shortly* ('before it be very shortly'). Rather than *ten times waar* ('ten times worse'), you find *waar be ten times ower* ('worse by ten times over').

This tendancy is extremely difficult to qualify, even though it is vividly familiar to me from conversations I have heard taking place between older relatives. In a humorous anecdote, the speaker will often shake their head and almost mutter the punchline in as indirect a way as they can come up with. This is cultural rather than linguistic, and is not unique to Cumbria. I have a feeling it may be related to the concept of *exformation*: information that is deliberately not stated because it is clear from context or from a shared cultural knowledge.

---

[16] German separable-prefix verbs are the equivalent of phrasal verbs in English (like 'turn off,' 'take on'), but they work slightly differently. The preposition is glued to the front of the verb; so the preposition *auf* ('up') can be attached to the verb *nehmen* ('to take') to form the verb *aufnehmen* ('to pick (something) up'). The preposition can then be detached from the verb and moved to a different part of a clause, e.g. *ich nehme es auf* ('I'm picking it up'), but the meaning of the verb is still altered by its relationship with the preposition. These are a pain in the arse for non-native speakers to learn, both in German and in English.

In this case, the engagement of the listener may be required to completely decode what is said by the storyteller. This fosters and reinforces social connections in a more immediate way than a straightforwardly-told story would.

I will finish off with another observation by Brilioth from 1913. In the preface of his *Grammar*, he describes the kind of bidialectalism that he observed in Cumbrians at the time:

> '...the whole character of the dialect serves to constitute it as a language of its own, quite distinct from standard English, both as regards phonology and vocabulary, and the natives are, in a way, distinctly bilingual, that is to say, if a true Cumbrian speaks his own dialect, he prides himself on speaking it quite pure and unmixed, [he talks real Cumbrian], but, on the other hand, if he [talks proud][17], i.e. standard English, you will frequently catch him using words derived from his native idiom instead of those belonging to polite English.'

This is a comment on the behaviour of Cumbrians in relation to their language, and it is very telling, particularly as Brilioth was not a local by any means, and had no reason to lie in order to characterise the dialect as more divergent from standard English than it was.

Börje Brilioth was a Swedish journalist and linguist, born in Östergötland in 1884. He was 29 when he wrote *A Grammar of the Dialect of Lorton* in 1913.

S. Dickson-Brown was a Cumbrian philologist. He wrote his supplement to William Dickinson's *Glossary of the Dialect of Cumberland* in 1905 alongside Edward William Prevost.

---

[17] The parts of this quote that I have put in square brackets were written by Brilioth in Cumbrian, in phonetic transcription.

Incorporation of Old Norse.

Because this chapter will deal with a time period well before that which this book focuses on, I will only go into a shallow level of detail. This topic will require further study at another time, and there may be existing literature on it that I have not read.

Famously, northern English dialects bear a certain amount of influence from Old Norse, the language spoken in medieval Scandinavia and associated with the Vikings. During the 800s AD, several Viking attacks took place on the north-eastern coast. A large portion of northern and eastern England was under Scandinavian control for some centuries after that, and was known as the Danelaw.

During these centuries, Scandinavian settlers (probably more peacefully than their Viking predecessors) flooded into northern England from various angles; some came directly by the east coast, others travelled through northern Scotland, Ireland and the Isle of Man, eventually reaching what is now Cumbria.

The extent to which Norse speakers interacted with and influenced their Anglo-Saxon neighbours is debated, but I am convinced that interaction on a colloquial level must have been very widespread; this is the only way of accounting for the scale of Norse influence on northern dialects.

To give some perspective on the issue: normally, when loan words are transferred from one language to another, they do not join the **core vocabulary** of the recipient language. That is, they rarely replace the most commonly-used words in the language. Even today, centuries after the Norman invasion and with intervening years of influence from ecclesiastical and scientific Latin, there are relatively few Romance words in the core vocabulary of a standard English speaker. I have been writing in fairly academic English here, yet more than 60% of the words in this chapter, up to the start of this sentence, have been natively Anglo-Saxon. In regular speech, this percentage would be markedly higher.

French words do not very often penetrate to our core vocabulary, because despite French being the language of law and royalty, it was not very widely spoken amongst ordinary people, even after the Norman invasion.

In contrast to this, Old Norse loan words have entered the core vocabulary of even standard English to a great extent, giving us everyday words like *them, their, take, ugly, skull, egg, skill, sale, skirt, gift, trust, bull, dirt, bug, muck* and *rotten*. They have seeped further into the core vocabulary of Cumbrian, giving a very broad array of everyday words which Brilioth lists in his *Grammar*, and some of which I will repeat at the end of this section.

The only explanation for such widespread transfer of core vocabulary is that people were interacting with Old Norse speakers on a day-to-day basis, sometimes marrying them and probably raising children that were bilingual - native speakers of both Northumbrian Old English and Old Norse. Even those communities or individuals that were not bilingual - which may have been the majority, as we do not see creolisation of the two languages - must have been able to understand a certain amount of conversational Old Norse.

A pertinent question here, which has been raised by many others, is that of how mutually intelligible the relevant dialects of Old Norse and Old English were. They were closely related languages anyway, but were they close enough that speakers of one could understand the other without making special effort to learn it?

Eric Martin Gay, in his 2014 thesis *Old English & Old Norse: an Enquiry into Intelligibility & Categorisation Methodology*, comes to the conclusion that there probably was some level of mutual intelligibility. Dr Jackson Crawford, in a YouTube video on the same subject, argues that they were probably not immediately mutually intelligible, but that it would not have been too taxing for a speaker of one to learn the other enough to get by. I lean more towards the latter, if only because I think the only reason there is so much mutual intelligibility between modern English dialects is that we are exposed to a variety of accents from a young age, and intuitively learn the correspondences between them.

When one language takes loan words from another, the loan words are usually converted from the phonology of the donor language into the phonology of the recipient language. Think of *spaghetti*, a loan word taken by English from Italian. When English speakers say *spaghetti*, we generally do not pronounce it as an Italian person would; we approximate it using the sounds that we would normally use in English. This same process happens in almost all languages that take loan words, because it would be impractical to expand a language's phonemic inventory by two or three phonemes every time it took a loan word, and it is difficult for speakers to jump out of the phonological system they are used to just to pronounce one or two words.

We must assume that the same thing happened when Old Norse loan words were adopted by Old English. Although we cannot see the everyday interactions of the communities in which this happened, we can tell something about the loaning process by looking at what lexical sets Old Norse loan words have fallen into in later Cumbrian. This may also give us hints about the finer details of the pronunciation of the dialects between which the loaning took place.

Brilioth provides us with a good source of these words, with helpful phonetic transcriptions and potential Scandinavian cognates. While some very clear patterns may be drawn, there are numerous Old Norse sounds that have multiple courses of development to later Cumbrian with no apparent rules governing them. This is perhaps inevitable, with several different regional varieties of Old Norse blending with several different regional varieties of Old English. It is not just regional variation that will have muddied the waters here. Diachronic variation - change through time - will also have complicated things. Sound changes may have happened in continental Scandinavia between one generation of migrants and the next. These sound changes do not have to have been very substantial to have affected how loan words were taken. Bear in mind that it was Old East Norse that was largely spoken on the east coast, and Old West Norse (potentially influenced by any number of Celtic languages) on the west coast of England. While we can expect most loan words into Cumbrian to be from Old West Norse, loans from East Norse may have come in via north-eastern dialects of English, clouding their pronunciation.

The short vowels have mostly been incorporated into exactly the lexical sets you would expect: Old Norse *a* becomes later Cumbrian /ɐ/, *e* becomes /e/, *u* becomes /ʊ/. Both *i* and *y* become /ɪ/ in later Cumbrian. Old English made a distinction between short /i/ and /y/, so presumably these vowels entered the language as two lexical sets, merging when the Old English vowels did.

Interestingly, Norse *ǫ* gives later Cumbrian /ɐ/ very regularly. This requires more careful examination. In Old English texts, wherever an *a* came before a nasal consonant, like *n* or *m*, writers seemed to use it interchangeably with the letter *o*. For example, the word *land* could be spelled either *land* or *lond*. The usual interpretation of Old English *a* is that it was /ɑ/ in most positions. This interchangeability before a nasal suggests that, in that environment, the sound changed in some way to become more like Old English *o* - for example, by rounding to /ɒ/. The Old Norse letter *ǫ* is thought to have represented a rounded, relatively open vowel, such as /ɔ/ or /ɒ/. With this in mind, the conflation makes sense. It may be that, in the relevant dialects, Old Norse *ǫ* sounded more like Old English rounded *a* than *o*.

Old Norse *ar* and *er* both become /ɐːr/, as expected. *Au* becomes /ɐʊ/. *Ei* and *ey* both seem to become /ɛː/. These diphthongs were different Old West Norse, being something like /ei/ and /øy/ respectively. The latter of these is the rounded equivalent of the former, and their conflation in the mind of a Northumbrian Old English speaker is easy to imagine. Alternatively, it may be that in the relevant variety of Old West Norse, which had already been spoken for a brief period in Ireland, these diphthongs had nearly or entirely merged anyway.

Norse *ó* gives later Cumbrian /ɪʊ/, suggesting that it was interpreted as the equivalent of Old English *ō*.

Old Norse was an inflected language, meaning extra bits and pieces could be added to words to mark case, gender and so on.

Most Cumbrian words descended from Old Norse roots show no evidence of this inflection. To me, this suggests that the speakers taking on the loan words recognised these bits as inflections and selectively removed them, which in turn suggests they had a good understanding of Old Norse syntax that doesn't come from just hearing the odd word and copying it.

This would have been more intuitive at the time, because Old English was also a highly inflected language, so speakers might have unconsciously recognised certain things as inflections just because a lot of words ended with them.

Old English nouns, like in many other languages, had **grammatical gender**. This was unrelated to gender in the social sense; an object could have feminine connotations (for example, it might be a female article of clothing) and have masculine gender, or vice versa. It was really just a way of categorising nouns. Nouns could be **masculine, feminine** or **neuter**, just like in modern German, and there was usually nothing about the structure or sound of a word that told you what gender it was. For each individual word, you just had to know.

The way grammatical gender manifested was through inflections applied to adjectives and articles surrounding the noun. The word *brocc* ('badger') was masculine, so if you wanted to write *the black badger*, you had to use the correct versions of the words *the* and *black*: in this case, you would say *se sweart brocc*. On the other hand, the word *gāt* ('goat') was feminine, so if you wanted to say *the black goat*, it would have to be *sēo swearte gāt*. This grammatical gender would have been a complex thing to learn, and it wasn't necessary to use grammatical gender correctly in order to be understood. If I learnt German without grammatical gender, a native speaker would still understand me - I would just sound like a foreigner.

This has led some people to the conclusion that it was Old Norse influence that caused grammatical gender to disappear in English, because Scandinavians could not be bothered to learn all of the necessary inflections and variations of the definite article. The loss of inflection and the levelling of conjugation · both seem to have started in the north of England and made their way south.

I am not sure where I stand on this idea. Old Norse had grammatical gender which corresponded closely to that of Old English, but that would not necessarily have made articles much easier to get the hang of; the definite article in O.N worked differently to that in O.E, having a different form and etymology and often being affixed to the end of the noun.

However, grammatical gender can disappear as a result of regular internal processes. Adjective endings were a hefty part of what marked grammatical gender in Old English, and these were usually unstressed, because stress in Germanic languages falls on the root. As a result, these could have been eroded away without external influence. The simplification of other aspects of grammatical gender has happened in numerous languages without the same level of interaction as O.N had on O.E.

Here is an edited and slightly abridged version of Brilioth's list of Cumbrian words of Old Norse origin. The Old Norse (ON) meaning will only be given where it differs from the Cumbrian meaning.

Addle /ˈɐdl̩/ - To earn. From ON *ǫðlask* 'to acquire.'

Hag /hɐg/ - To chop, hew. ON *hǫgg-*.

Ansel /ˈɛnsl̩/ - The price of the first thing sold; a coin given to the wearer of new suit. ON *handsal* 'a transference of ownership from one to another by joining hands.'

Hank /ˈhɐŋk/ - A length of thread. ON *hǫnk*.

Arr /ɐːr/ - A scar. ON *err*.

Harber /ˈhɐːrbər/ - A room, place of reception. Related to the English *harbour*.

Arvel /ˈɐːrvəl/ - Relating to inheritance or funeral. Can be applied to food eaten at a funeral, cakes distributed at a funeral (*arvel breed*), etc. ON *erfiǫl*.

How /hɐʊ/ - A hill or hillock. ON *haugr*.

Hain /hɛːn/ - To leave a pasture field unused until grass grows again. ON *hegna* 'to enclose within a fence, preserve.'

Bang /bɐŋ/ - To beat. OWN *banga*.

Batten /ˈbɐtən/ - To fatten. ON *batna* 'to improve.'

Bain /bɛːn/ - (Of a path) handy, accommodating. ON *beinn* 'straight, direct.'

Bait /bɛːt/ - Food eaten whilst on the road or at work. Possibly from ON *beit* 'pasture'.

Big /bɪg/ - Barley. ON *bygg*.

Blaik /blɛːk/ - Pale, yellow, washed-out. ON *bleikr* - Jackson Crawford convincingly argues that in Old Norse, this word referred to warm colours that were not considered to be 'optimal' - that is, duller reds and yellows, or the colour of low-quality gold. It should be noted that the way colour is categorised varies hugely from language to language, and Old Norse classified colours differently to Modern English.

Brandreth /ˈbrɛndrəθ/ - A three-legged iron frame used in open hearths to support a baking plate. ON *brandreið* 'grate.'

Briukt /briʊkt/ - (Of a sheep) having interspersed black and white hair on the legs and face. Modern Cumbrian shepherds consider this kind of pattern to be unattractive in a sheep, and will try to separate the two colours by plucking out errant hairs before sheep are taken to a show or auction. While Brilioth gives no attested ON origin, he gives the modern Swedish *brokig* ('mottled') and dialectal Norwegian and Swedish *brók* ('pied'). This points to an Old Norse form with a backed, rounded, mid or open vowel, which would give the later Cumbrian form we see.

Dowly /ˈdɛʊlɪ/ - (Of a place) lonely, desolate. Brilioth gives ON *dǫufligr*, but I cannot find this anywhere.

Drukken /ˈdrʊkən/ - Drunk. Probably from the ON *drukkinn*, the past participle of *drekka* 'to drink.'

Heft /heft/ - (Usually in past participle form as **heftit**, applied to sheep) instinctually attached to a particular fell or piece of land, so that they will attempt to get back to it if they are taken away from it. ON *hefta* 'to bind, hold back.'

Egg /eg/ - An egg. Worthy of note because it was originally considered a northern word (with the southern form being *ey*). People with a long-standing interest in the history of English will know a story recounted by William Caxton in 1490, in which a northern merchant approaches a southern woman in a marketplace and asks her for some eggs. The woman replies that she cannot speak French. The misunderstanding continues until one of the man's friends translates for him. Now *ey* is obsolete, and *egg* is the standard English word. ON *egg*.

Elden /'eldən/ - Fuel. ON *eldr* 'fire.'

Farantly /'ferənt̩lɪ/ - Fashionable, respectable. Possibly related to ON *fara* 'to travel.' The present participle form *farandi*, which would give Cumbrian *farand*, would have meant 'travelling.' A semantic change from this to 'fashionable' is conceivable, but this one is possibly clutching at straws a bit.

Fell /fel/ - A mountain or upland hill. ON *fell*.

Fwors /fwɔːrs/ - A waterfall, as in several place names, including *Aira force*. ON *fors*.

Garn /gɐːrn/ - Yarn. ON *garn*. Brilioth notes that it exists alongside a natively English form *yarn*, 'a story.'

Garth /gɐːrθ/ - A yard or enclosure. ON *garðr*. Those familiar with Norse mythology may recognise this as a cognate of the ending of the word *Asgard* (ON *Ásgarðr*).

Gauk /gɐʊk/ - A cuckoo. ON *gaukr*.

Gaul /gɐʊl/ - To howl, bellow. OWN *gaula*.

Gaupen /'gɐʊpən/ - The amount that can be held in two hands with the palms open. Probably related to the OE word *gēap* 'broad, open', but that would give Cumbrian **yeep*, so it cannot be a direct descendent. Far more likely to be from an ON cognate **gaup(n)*. The *Etymological Dictionary of Proto-Germanic* (see further reading) mentions an ON form *gaupn* 'both hands held together.'

Gaut /gɐʊt/ - A boar. Can be used as an insult for a man who behaves like a boar. ON *goltr*.

Gyat /gjɐt/ - A path, way. Found in many northern street names in the form *-gate*. ON *gata*, of the same meaning. In the Middle English period, non-high vowels in stressed open syllables were lengthened. The word *nama* gained a long vowel and gave us the modern *name*. *Gata* did the same thing, joining the *stone* lexical set and giving later Cumbrian /gjɐt/.

Gill /gɪl/ - A ravine, usually with a stream in it. ON *gil*.

Gilt /gɪlt/ - A young sow used for breeding. ON *gyltr*.

Gimmer /ˈgɪmər/ - A female sheep less than two years old. ON *gymbr*, 'a young female sheep.' Note the regular disappearance of the plosive /b/ after the nasal /m/.

Grise /grɐɪs/ - Young pig; wild boar. Obsolete by Brilioth's time apart from in place names, such as *Mungrisdale*. ON *gríss*.

Graidly /ˈgrɛːdlɪ/ - Good, proper. ON *greiðligr*, 'prepared.'

Graip /grɛːp/ - A dung-fork. ON *greip*, which Brilioth notes is only known from Old Norse in the sense of the noun 'grasp,' or the part of the hand used for grasping. He also notes that modern Scandinavian descendents of this word have the same meaning as the Cumbrian, so the Old Norse word may have had an additional sense that was never written down (after all, I am not sure how many times dung-forks are mentioned in the sagas).

Kail /kɐɪl/ - A boil, sore. ON *kýli*.

Karl /kɐːrl/ - A coarse, common man. Used in the term *carlen sark* ('working shirt'). ON *karl*, 'a man' - alternatively, an unpalatalised form of OE *ceorl*.

Kowp /kɐʊp/ - To exchange. ON *kaupa,* 'to buy.' Cognate with the English word *cheap*.

Keld /keld/ - A water spring. ON *kelda*.

Kittel /ˈkɪtl̩/ - To tickle. ON *kitla*.

Kod /kɒd/ - A pillow, hassock, pin cushion. ON *koddi*.

Kriuk /kriʊk/ - A shepherd's crook. ON *krókr* 'hook.'

Lait /lɐɪt/ - To *lait on* somebody is to trust them. ON *hlíta* 'to trust.'

Lowp /lɐʊp/ - To leap, jump. ON *hlaupa* 'to jump.'

Laik /lɛːk/ - To play, joke. ON *leika*.

Lairy /ˈlɛːrɪ/ - Covered in mud or clay. ON *leir* 'mud, clay.'

Lait /ˈlɛːt/ - To search for, to bring. ON *leita* 'to look for.'

Lee /liː/ - A scythe. ON *lé*.

Lyath /ljɐθ/ - A barn. Possibly related to ON *hlaða* 'to stack, build.' Presumably subject to the same vowel lengthening as *gata*.

Melder /ˈmeldər/ - The amount of grain ground at a given time. ON *meldr* 'flour.' This is a rare example of a Cumbrian word that has retained a fossilised version of the Old Norse nominative singular ending -*r*.

Midden /ˈmɪdən/ - A heap of manure. No recorded Old Norse cognate, but Scandinavian cognates listed by Brilioth all end in *-ng*. This is an interesting example of a word which is clearly of northern dialectal origin, having come from Old Norse and dropped what was presumably a final /g/, but has entered mainstream (and even academic) English in an archaeological context.

Mun /mʊn/ - Must. ON *munu*, 'shall, will.'

Naut /nɐʊt/ - Cattle. ON *naut* 'bull.' Cognate with the Old English form *nēat*.

Nae /nɛː/ - No. ON *nei*. This is is contrast with the forms /niə/ (OE *nā*) and /niː/ (OE *nē*), which also exist.

Oam /ɔːm/ - An elm tree. ON *almr*.

Raik /rɛːk/ - To stray or wander around a large area. ON *reik* 'wandering.'

Riust /riʊst/ - Praised, commended. ON *hrós*, 'praise.'

Rug /rʊg/ - To shake, pull roughly. ON *rugga* , 'to shake.'

Sakless /ˈsɐkləs/ - Simple, stupid, weak-minded, pathetic. ON *saklauss*, 'innocent.'

Sark /sɐːrk/ - Shirt. ON *serkr*. This root also gives the English word *berserk*, from the Norse word *berserkr*, which means either *bear-shirt* or *bare-shirt* (interpreted as meaning that these people were known for wearing bear skins, or for wearing less than usual, at least while fighting). This sense of the word has nothing to do with the Cumbrian descendent, though, which just means *shirt*.

Saut /sɐʊt/ - Various diseases or imbalances in cattle. The specific disease to which this was applied may have varied from region to region. The origin of this word is difficult to gauge, as it matches the expected reflex of neither the OE word *suht* ('illness') nor the ON word *sott*. The Norse word had originally been *soht, prior to the assimilation of *-ht* clusters to *-tt* (see OE *þuhte* vs. ON *þóttr*). Brilioth suggests that the Norse word was incorporated into English before this assimilation: the form *soht would reliably give Cumbrian /sɐʊt/.

Skarf /skɐːrf/ - A cormorant. OWN *skarfr*.

Skemmel /ˈskeməl/ - A long, backless bench. ON *skemill*.

Skratty /ˈskrɛtɪ/ - The name of a goblin-like thing that was thought to haunt fellsides, making frightening sounds. ON *skratti*, a word applied to a folkloric wizard or goblin, cognate with German *Schrat*, a term for the 'moss people' of folk stories. More on this can be found in the chapter on folklore.

Slape /slɛːp/ - Slippery or smooth, sometimes used of a cleanly-shaven face. ON *sleipr*.

Sliuth-dog /slɪʊθdɔg/ - A bloodhound. Probably the origin of the standard English *sleuth* ('detective'). ON *slóð*, 'track, way.'

Slokken /ˈslɒknn̩/ - To quench thirst. ON *slokna,* 'to be extinguished.'

Snape /snɛːp/ - To snub or restrain. Used of a farm-hand who has been given useless work to keep him busy. ON *sneypa*, 'to dishonour or disgrace.'

Stang /stɛŋ/ - A pole, stake, fencepost. OWN *stǫng*.

Stanger /ˈstɛŋər/ - A wasp. Resembles ON *stanga*, the indefinite genitive plural of *stǫng* - in other words, 'of stakes.' Presumably related in some way to the wasp's sting.

Stape /stɛːp/ - To *stape something up* is to overturn it. ON *steypa*, 'to overturn or upset.'

Steg /steg/ - A gander (male goose). ON *steggr*, related to English 'stag.'

Swang /swɛŋ/ - A wet, boggy hollow in the middle of pasture land. ON *svangr*, 'thin, emaciated, empty.'

Tarn /tɛːrn/ - A small, often glacial lake. ON *tjǫrn*.

Clip /klɪp/ - To shear sheep. ON *klippa*.

Tup /tʊp/ - A ram (male sheep). No direct ON root given by Brilioth, but several clear cognates in Scandinavian languages.

Ugly /ˈʊglɪ/ - Ugly, probably a northern word before it became a southern one. OWN *uggligr* 'fearsome.'

Wai /wɛɪ/ - A cow who has born no calves and is less than three years old. ON *kvíga*. Subject to the same change as *what, when, wheen*.

Warda /ˈwɛːrdə/ - Week day or working day. ON *hverr dagr*, 'a working day; a day that is not a holiday.'

Cumbrian Culture.

This section is likely to be the longest in the book, but no segment of a book can adequately describe an entire culture. It should be clear to anybody who has read older Cumbrian literature that to be immersed in the culture is to have a mindset and an understanding of the world subtly, sometimes substantially, different from that of a modern person in the south of England. Aspects of such rural culture surely hang on in other parts of the rural north, as well as in Scotland (where even the metropolitan culture is worlds apart from that of England), Northern Ireland and Wales (likewise), and the West Country. Any comment I make on it will necessarily be subjective, so I would encourage the reader to bear in mind that I have been raised in the south of England in the 21st century (albeit with several Cumbrian family members), and that my experience of the culture is not going to be the same as that of a modern fell-farmer, or of a travelling salesman from the 1700s, or of a schoolteacher from the 1940s. On the other hand, I would encourage the reader to suspend any preconceived ideas they may have about the north of England as a place of smog and factory workers. These are stereotypes, and would probably not be recognised by most people living in Cumbria over the last four centuries.

Quite aside from the 'industrial north' stereotypes, another set of preconceived ideas is often at play in the study of lake district culture. As both James Rebanks and Terry McCormick have written extensively about in *A Shepherd's Life* and *Lake District Fell Farming* respectively, poetic traditions over the last three hundred-or-so years have firmly established a romantic idea of the lake district that bears no resemblance to the landscape as seen from the perspective of the fell-farmer. Poets like Wordsworth and Wainwright have described it as an idyll and place of escape and innocence, made comparisons between Cumbrian shepherds and the biblical image of a shepherd. Even as somebody who has not been directly involved in fell farming and has mainly experienced Cumbrian farming culture only through the experiences, behaviour and habits of my older relatives, there seems to me to be no remote echo of actual Cumbrians in these descriptions. Descriptions of them are reductive, and often make no attempt to actually represent them in their own right, but as analogies or poetic devices.

Rural Cumbria, until staggeringly late-on, was a place in which people subsisted off of their own land for a great part of what they ate, wore and used. Into the early 20th century, people largely made their own clothes, which was unusual at that point in England. Not only did they make their own clothes; they did so from scratch. They used wool from their own sheep, or linen from their own flax. People made and repaired their own tools. They grew their own vegetables and, of course, raised their own livestock. Doing any of these things on a small-scale was not unheard of anywhere in England at that time, but almost total reliance on them was unusual. If a given hamlet had somehow become entirely isolated, they could have carried on indefinitely of their own accord.

Despite this self-reliance, the area has always had a complex economy. Given the upland terrain of most of central Cumbria (the area now called the Lake District), it is best suited to sheep grazing, and this is arguably the root of the local culture. The fells are agriculturally inhospitable, with wildly unpredictable weather, rough terrain and very little to eat. The valleys and lowlands, although not especially cold in the grand scheme of things, have experienced snow drifts several feet in height. Last winter, at the time of writing, some drifts entirely covered up doorways and there were reports of people burning their own furniture[18].

The Herdwick, a breed almost totally unique to the fells, is quite capable of thriving in these sorts of conditions. James Rebanks, in *The Shepherd's Life*, describes an instance of a Herdwick surviving buried underneath a snow drift for more than two days, chewing its own wool. The Herdwick is born black, becomes

---

[18] When I told my now-late grandmother about this over the phone, she commented that they were 'daft people.'

slate-grey after its first clipping, and the fleece becomes lighter as it ages. The face of an adult Herdwick is generally white.

As in other areas where upland farming is traditionally practiced, the stock spend a lot of their time grazing freely on the fells; they are loose for the entirety of winter to forage their own food. No restriction has to be imposed on them because they are *heftit*: they naturally know to remain in a certain area, and will try to return to that area if taken away from it. The sheep and the shepherd have a complicated relationship, mediated by the dog (usually a border collie).

The *Memorandum of Old Times*, published in 1869, is a highly useful resource for reconstructing Cumbrian culture in the late 18th and early 19th centuries, describing a time 'when George III was King.' It is written in simple poetic verse, with four lines per stanza, presumably in the author's own dialect. It goes through the year month-by-month, beginning with an introductory segment set in winter, where it remarks that people *hardly stir't out o' t'neuk* (lit. 'hardly stirred out of the nook'). Here, *neuk* ('nook') appears to refer to a house. It states that people did little outdoor work in winter, aside from collecting peat. It paints a picture of people as idle and bored, scraping by and with little to do. They would make clothes, thresh, card wool and so on, but the only outdoor work mentioned is the collection of turfs (peat) from the fells. This was used for burning, and for making 'raddle,' a dye applied to the wool of sheep about to be taken to auction. The reason for the application of raddle is not entirely clear, even to some fell-farmers.

The *Memorandum* gives us a bit of information about clothing in the early 19th century;

> *A carlin sark new was rumplement gear*
> *To wear next a maisterman's skin,*
> *So he lent it to t'sarvant to beetle an' wear*
> *By way of a brekkin in.*

> *T'oald fwok were drist i duffel blue.*
> *And t'youngsters i heamm-spun grey,*
> *And nowder were often ower clean or new -*

Bit darn't frae day to day.

Although a lot of the language here is influenced by standard
influence, we see strong hints of typical Cumbrian
pronunciation; *gear* is rhymed with *wear* (at this point, probably
/ˈgiː‿ər/ and /ˈwiː‿ər/), and *drist* is spelled with 'i', reflecting the
inconsistency in other works because the actual realisation of the
vowel hangs on the boundary between /e/ and /ɪ/.

These stanzas claim that it was usual for a *sarvant* (employee,
servant) to wear a *carlin sark* (working shirt) in before giving it
to the *maister* (employer, master) to wear, because a new shirt
was too rough for an employer. It also puts forward that older
people wore blue, and younger people wore grey. It's unclear
whether this refers to the working-shirt or to an outer woollen
coat-like garment; *heamm-spun* (home-spun) could refer to
either, as both linen and wool were said to be *spun*. It notes that
the garments were rarely seen fresh, but repaired on a daily
basis. Their shoes were coated in ferns and straw.

The author then describes their winter eating habits. They had
poddish ('porridge') in the morning, and at midday had a meal
called *taty and point*. In his *Glossary of Words and Phrases*,
William Dickinson describes this meal; especially poor people
would have a plate of mashed potatoes, and in the middle of the
table would have a piece of butter or fat on a plate in the middle
of the table. People could point their potato-laden forks at the fat,
but were not allowed to touch it. More porridge was then had in
the evening.

At Martinmas - the 11th of November - a cow was killed and cut
into four. One piece was retained by its owners, and the other
three given to neighbours. The *Memorandum* suggests that this is
one of the three times a year that meat was generally consumed,
the other two being *Kersmas* (Christmas) and *Clippin* (shearing).
This excludes bacon, which it suggests was consumed
occasionally. I cannot comment on the accuracy of this, or how
widespread it might have been; it doesn't seem out-of-the-
question that meat was eaten more often than this.

Bread, it says, was *clap-keakk meadd o' barley meal / Or hard*

havver bannock so thick. In other words, it was made from
barley or oats. Both *keakk* and *bannock* suggest a sort of cake:
bannock is not a word unique to Cumbrian, and elsewhere in the
literature describes a kind of sweet cake with dried fruit.
It was typical to drink sour-milk or, occasionally, *treacle beer.* I
would add to this by saying that *yal* (beer) is mentioned
numerous times in numerous different stories and ballads and, at
least in the 19th century (almost certainly earlier), it was in no
short supply to most people. Cider was not unheard-of. Despite
its cultural and geographic proximity to Scotland, and the
county's abundance of peat (which was certainly used by the
locals), dialect literature does not mention whisky very much.
While it undoubtedly existed in Cumbria at the time, perhaps it
was not held in higher regard than any other British-produced
spirit available at the time.
The author then moves on to January, beginning it with a brief
(if anachronistic) description of *Kersenmas* (Christmas).
Whether this is because Christmas was thought to spill over into
the new year, or just because he had not had the opportunity to
talk about it before, is not obvious. He touches on feasting, and
mentions people staying up late at night, drinking and dancing.
The stanza after that seems to describe what can only be the
hangover the morning after Christmas;

> *They woken next mwornin and find theirsels queer,*
> *And o' out o' sworts for hard wark,*
> *Bit Kersemas comes nobbet yance in a year,*
> *And measst on't is kent efter dark.*

The last line (*and most of it is known after dark*) could either
refer to the fact days in winter are relatively short, or to the fact
that even on Christmas, work would still have to be done during
the day while it was light. The wording of the next stanza is
probably my favourite, and I will give a full translation
underneath;

> *Wi' snow a feutt thick – mebby clean out o' cwols,*
> *"Keaa fetch a pack-lead on a horse.*

> *"Pick t'best rwoad ther is, and mind keep out o' t'whols,*
> *"Lest thou torfor ont' moor, and 's a corse."*

With snow a foot thick – maybe fresh out of coals,
"[???], put a pack-load on a horse.
"Pick the best road there is, and mind to keep out of the holes,
"In case you perish on the moor, and are a corpse."

Fetch has a broader meaning than in standard English, and can
be used to mean *put*. This may well be an innovation in the
north-west; I'm not aware of any instances of *feccan* being used
in this way in Old English. It can also be used in the sense *to be
fetched up* ('to be brought up'), e.g. *aa were fetcht up i
Cumberland.* The latter part of the stanza is an example of the
very passive attitude, found throughout Cumbrian literature,
towards the harshness of life in the rural north-west at this time.
Remember that the author is describing a period between the late
1700s and early 1800s; any vehicle sturdier than a horse and
cart, or a horse and trap, was unheard-of. In this case, no cart is
mentioned at all. If the horse dropped dead or became injured in
an inopportune place, the rider's chances of survival might be
slim, especially during the night. When compacted snow was a
foot deep, snow drifts might have been seven or eight foot deep
in certain places, obscuring visibility.
The author makes rare use of a footnote here, noting that guide-
lights were often hung on gates 'before commons were enclosed,
or roads were made.' This should not be taken to imply that there
were no tracks; only that there were no well-maintained roads.
The author turns to February, and describes threshing and *deeten*
(winnowing). *Deet* comes ultimately from Old English *dihtan*,
and has developed parallel to *neet* and *seet*; the modern English
reflex would be *dight*. Some threshed and winnowed wheat grain
is put aside for frummety, a porridge-like dish made from
cracked wheat and either milk or meat stock. This was served in
a piggin with *a bit o' sote fish* - 'a bit of salt(ed) fish.'
The author uses the verb *cree* to describe the process by which
the wheat is cracked. Sure enough, Dickinson's glossary gives
cree as meaning 'to crush or break into fragments.' I have tried

briefly to determine the etymology of this, but I cannot find any obvious source in Old English, nor any cognates in other West Germanic varieties. The word would probably have had a palatal fricative [ç] at the end, in parallel with *neet, hee* and so on. It may come from an unattested Old English root; something like **crihan*.

Cannelmas is briefly touched upon. The word *cannel* is what we would expect as a cognate of standard English *candle*; it shows the deletion of a plosive after a nasal and before an unstressed vowel, as we see in *brimmel, spinnel, anger, langer*.

One stanza in the section on February goes into some detail about the role of women; they spun wool or linen, it says, and sang while they did it. We do not find much more about women for a while; much of the text is concerned with the agricultural tasks carried out by men, although I doubt very much that women were not involved in such tasks, considering the man-power (no pun intended) required to undertake them.

The section on March is primarily focused on ploughing; it claims that the plough was home-made from blackthorn (*roan tree*), with very scant iron attachments. One stanza described the sorts of pack animals that might be employed in ploughing; *lang-hornt owsen two pair* is tricky to interpret. It could be that *two pair* just refers to a single pair (with the word *two* reinforcing the meaning of the word *pair*) or, perhaps more likely, it could be that four oxen were used in total, with only two working at any given time. Alternatively, *two lang-tailed horse unshod* ('two long-tailed horses without shoes') were used. The struggle of the *plue hodder* ('plough holder') is then outlined. Ploughing with animals (although I have not done it myself) must have been an agitating task, and that is what the *Memorandum* tells us. You are working with two very hefty animals, trying to control them and drive them in a certain direction whilst holding the plough stable. Every so often you will hit a stone, and will have to re-adjust. The plough-holder apparently *sweers* and says *uncanny words* throughout the ordeal; one of a couple of references to swearing that we find in Cumbrian literature.

Another is at the end of *Bobby Banks' Bodderment,* which I will analyse in detail later; when Bobby returns home from the market, he realises he has forgotten something important. The story ends thus;

> *"Od's wuns an' deeth, that's what I' forgitten!"*
> *That was what I said. What Betty said I think I willn't tell ye.*

Bobby first writes a 'minced oath' out in full; he clearly considers this to be less severe than what Betty subsequently says. It's clear, then, that both men and women swore in some way, in certain circumstances, in a way that was more extreme than minced oaths. The nature of these swear words is lost to us, because they were never printed.

Of the ploughing, it's important to bear in mind how cold it still would have been in March. There might well still be snow on the ground, it might be frost-hardened. Alternatively, depending on the year, it might have been a mess of mud and slush. In a later stanza, the author mentions fierce wind and sleet. It is no wonder that after the unpleasantness of ploughing, people would go home and have a warm meal; fried grey peas, grain and oats is the example given. People would sit around the hearth as the storms blew outside, and drops of soot trickled in from the chimney. The author gives us a surprisingly relatable account of the finer details of farm life at this time.

After the frost, in April, oats (*haver*) would be sown, as well as linen with which to make clothes after it was harvested. Potatoes were planted, as well. It goes on a little tangent, here;

> *Bit peelin' o' taties was thought a girt sham,*
> *An t'prentice was setten to scrapin;*
> *Nea doubt he thought scrapin was nought but a 'bam,'*
> *And was laid onto him as a snapin.*
>
> *Than he wad git drowsy, and noddle and scrape,*
> *As an unpaid prentice wad dee;*
> *His knife and his taty would seun git so slape*
> *They wad rowl out o' hand off his knee.*

But peeling of potatoes was thought a great shame,
And the apprentice was told to scrape them;
No doubt he thought scraping was only a joke,
Which was given to him as a snub.

Then he would get drowsy, and half-fall-asleep as he scraped,
As an unpaid apprentice will do;
His knife and potato would soon get so smooth
They would roll out of his hand off his knee.

Slape, here used to mean *smooth,* is derived from the Old Norse word *sleipr* (smooth), as in *Sleipnir*, the name of Odin's eight-legged horse. Of course, it was a mundane word in most contexts, both in Cumbrian and in Old Norse.

Lambing time in late April and May is described as might be expected; people got very little sleep, and might have been needed to aid with the birth of a lamb at any point. This is one aspect of traditional sheep farming that has not changed to this day; lambing ewes require a lot of attention. While they are generally capable of lambing themselves, the infant mortality rates of wild sheep are obviously not desirable to farmers, and so effort must be taken to ensure as few lambs die during birth as possible.

There is a brief examination of the type of grasses used for kindling fires (the author mentions thistles and couch-grass) and what plants might be smoked in a pipe alongside tobacco (*cleet-leaf,* which I cannot find a translation for in any glossary), and then the author seems to note that tea, despite having been introduced to England nearly two centuries earlier, was considered a treat, in contrast to the habit of drinking it *three times a-day* that he suggests was about at the time of his writing. Whether he is contrasting late 18th-century Cumbria to mid 19th-century Cumbria, or to the south of England, he does not specify.

For June, he briefly says that the milking-cows were fed on ash saplings, and then launches into a description of market-time, which is also described (albeit more humorously) in *Bobby*

Banks' Bodderment. Both texts describe it as being a substantial trek away; people might travel for hours to get to market, even for more than a day. *Bodderment* names the market-town as Keswick, which has held that role for many centuries. It also says that Bobby's wife allows him to have dinner there, as well as a pint of beer. In the *Memorandum*, it seems the people are not quite as fortunate; in order to 'scrape and save the days takings,' they go without dinner, and have *nought bit three hoperth o' yal.* Presumably *hoperth* is the same as the southern English *ha'porth* (ha'penny's worth). I could not tell you how much beer three ha'pennies would have got you back then. The rest of the section addresses peat-cutting, which is done to this day in the fells. The peat may have been used in crop production, but also for 'raddling' sheep to give them a distinctive reddish colour before shows.

July is described as one of the more enjoyable months; first sheep and gathered and washed, and then, a *fortneet* later, they are clipped. Clipping was, and still is, an event of widespread importance. I will let the author speak for himself here.

> *Now gedder in t'sheep and wesh them in t'dem,*
> *And swing them and sop them in t'watter:*
> *If a waik'an sud torfer it's nobbut t'oald gem,*
> *And mebby it's nea girt matter.*
>
> *Sek bleatin o' lambs, and sek barkin o' dogs!*
> *Sek jybin and jwokin o' men!*
> *Sek clat'rin o' lads in their old cokert clogs!*
> *Sek drinkin o' whisky! Amen.*
>
> *Let sheep run a fortneet and than comes on clippin,*
> *And bleatin, and fleecin o' woo.*
> *They submit, without whimper, to tyin and strippin,*
> *And feel leetsome they hardly know how.*
>
> *Sek a gedd'rin o' clippers and helpers and that!*
> *Sek elbows, and clinkin o' shears!*
> *Sek sweatin! Sek crackin o' dogs, and o' what*
> *An income some woo-buyer clears!*

In the first of these four stanzas, the author writes *if a waik'an sud torfer it's nobbut t'oald gem / and mebby it's nea girt matter* ('if a weak one should die it's only the old game / and maybe it's no great matter'). This might seem surprising given he has previously said things that suggest his family were not well-off, but loss of sheep was certainly an occupational hazard. If you wander the fells for long enough today, you will eventually find a sheep that has died. The shepherd would soon know about it: unlike in some agricultural societies, where cattle are vital and sheep are of secondary importance, a good shepherd of the fells could supposedly recognise any of his sheep and knew them all individually. They knew how old they were, the state of their health and roughly how much they could sell for.

The shepherds would then have a lot of food and drink, sing a few songs from a selection they all knew off-by-heart, and go to sleep. Over the coming days, they might help neighbouring farmers in clipping if they had not done it yet.

The section on August describes the cutting of hay; in the hottest part of the day, the workers cannot work for for the horse-flies and the sun, so they go to sleep on the hay, and make it up by working 'at night'. I don't know what the practicalities of cutting hay in pitch darkness would have been. Perhaps it depended on the amount of moonlight available. My grandfather says that in his youth, hay-cutting was done until it got dark (about ten o'clock). Anybody who has worked on a farm with minimal artificial light (as I have in some small capacity) will know that darkness comes on quickly and often without anybody really noticing, and so it is conceivable that they just carried on working through it until somebody realised that they could no longer see what they were doing.

The author goes on for a few stanzas about the importance of keeping up work, which holds true in any agricultural community; if anybody slacks off for a day or two, he says, they are bound to find that something's gone wrong, and they will have to spend another day or two overstraining themselves to make up for it. The author gives the example of the roof needing to be repaired, in which case somebody would need to venture into the moor to gather something for makeshift thatch, *for strea's owwer costly a thing* ('because straw's too expensive'). The September section naturally focuses on harvest, but makes another mention of facial hair, the first having been very near the start of the poem. Men apparently shaved on a weekly basis, so that they were generally clean-shaven, but would build up a week's worth of growth before they shaved again. There is then another description of feasting at the end of the harvest season, not unlike the others. After this, the flax is harvested and bleached by lying it out on the grass, drying it completely. This can then be worked whenever anybody has a spare moment over the autumn and winter months, as is described at the start of the poem.

In October, it says, homes were visited by a *Whittlegeat* (presumably /ˈwɪtlgjɐt/) man, who would teach them reading and basic arithmetic. The *geat* component means *road,* which to me implies somebody who travels from place to place, rather than the children having to travel to him. John Pagen White expands upon this in his *Lays & Legends of the English Lake County* (2018), saying that 'Whittlegate' comprised a few weeks' worth of food, provided to a vicar or local teacher by the inhabitants of his parish. Each household provided a certain amount depending on what they had (a bit like a tax), and they alternated so that the vicar had these provisions throughout the year. A teacher may travel from place to place, and receive Whittlegate in return for his service. This does not say much of the prevelance of literacy in Cumbria in the early 1800s; one imagines certain households foregoing this teaching, either because they were too poor to justify the expenditure or because they did not feel it necessary for their children to be able to read or write.

And it wouldn't have been especially necessary, unless the children had ambitions outside of farming. The level of arithmetic required for livestock management is easily learnt by exposure to it, and reading would have been completely unnecessary outside of jobs that specifically required it. Stories and songs could be passed about by word of mouth, as could relevant information. Being able to write letters might have made life slightly more convenient.

The author talks about *soavin* of sheep. The word *soav* is certainly cognate with the standard English *salve*, and probably meant to medically treat a sheep with some substance; nowadays, this is called *dipping*. The author gives little information about how this was done, but it is now done by collecting the sheep from the fell and driving them one-by-one into a trough or bath filled with sheep dip, a formula of chemicals designed to prevent the sheep from developing fungal or parasitic diseases such as fly strike. Like clipping, the author says that farmers helped each other with this task, and that it could be an enjoyable affair and a chance to speak to other local shepherds.

The activities described in November start to resemble those discussed at the beginning of the poem again; preparation of wool and flax, for example, and threshing. Threshing was done with a flail; two wooden sticks held together by the ends with a chain, so that one stick can be held and the other swung and brought down onto the grain to separate it from the chaff (*caff* in Cumbrian because of the lack of palatisation). I asked my grandfather about flail threshing once. He said that it was not common practice anymore when he was a child, but that they as children sometimes made toy flails.

Children were sent to collect sheaves of stems to make candles from. Martinmas occurred, a cow was once again killed and divided between neighbours, and salmon were caught in the beck to be dried and eaten some way down the line.

In December, oats were dried in a kiln and milled to produce oatmeal, with seeds being collected to sow again. Wheat was winnowed (*deetit*) in a sieve or on a *deetin hill,* where it was thrown into the wind, which blew away the chaff and left the grain to fall back down. The wheat was then milled for bread. This is about as much as the *Memorandum* has to say, although I would recommend that you read it, as it contains a lot of finer details about peoples' feelings towards certain activities, and the visceral experiences of life in Cumbria at the time.

Josiah (or Joseph) Relph's 1747 *Miscellany of Poems* allows us some insight a bit further back. Relph was born in Sebergham in the north-east of what is now Cumbria, and lived between 1712 and 1743, with his poetry being published posthumously. Some of the poetry is written in literary English, some in Cumbrian. The first poem of the *Miscellany* is partially in standard English, but switches to Cumbrian a few lines in. I will give the poem in its original form, and then provide a translation of that portion of it which is written in Cumbrian.

When welcome rain the weary reapers drove
Beneath the shelter of a neighbouring grove,
Robin, a love-sick swain, lagg'd far behind,
Nor seem'd the weight of falling showers to mind;
A distant solitary shade he sought,
And thus disclos'd the troubles of his thought -

Ay, ay, thur drops may cuil my outside heat;
Thur callar blasts may wear the boilen sweat;
But my het bluid, my heart aw in a bruil,
Nor callar blasts can wear, nor drops can cuil.
Here, here it was (a wae light on the pleace)
'At first I gat a gliff o' Betty's feace.

Blind on this trod the smurker tripp'd, and theer
At the deail-head unluckily we shear;
Heedless I glimm'd, nor cou'd my een command,
Till gash the sickle went into my hand:

Down held the bluid; the shearers all brast out
In sweels o' laughter; Betty luik'd about;
Reed grew my fingers, reeder far my feace;
What cou'd I de in seck a dispert kease!

Away I sleeng'd, to grandy meade my mean,
My grandy (God be wud her now she's geane)
Skilfu' the gushen bluid wi' cobwebs staid,
Then on the sair a healen plaister laid;
The healen plaister eas'd the painful sair,

The arr indeed remains, but naething mair.

Not sae that other wound, that inward smart;
My grandy cou'd not cure a bleedin heart.
I've bworn the bitter torment three lang year,
And aw my life-time mun be fworc'd to bear,
'Less Betty will a kind physician pruive,
For nin but she has skill to medcin luive.

But how shou'd honest Betty give relief?
Betty's a perfet stranger to my grief.
Oft I've resolv'd my ailment to explain,
Oft I've resolv'd indeed - but all in vain:
A springin blush spred fast owr aither cheek,
Down Robin luik'd and deuce a word cou'd speak.

Can I forget that night? - I never can!
When on the clean-sweep'd hearth the spinnels ran;
The lasses drew their line wi' busy speed,
The lads as busy minded ev'ry thread;
When, sad! The line sae slender Betty drew,
Snap went the thread and down the spinnel flew.
To me it meade - the lads began to glop -
What cou'd I de? I mud, mud take it up.
I tuik it up and (what gangs pleaguy hard)
E'en reach'd it back without the sweet reward.

O lastin stain! e'en yet it's eith to treace
A guilty conscience in my blushen feace;
I fain wou'd wesh it out but never can.
Still fair it bides like bluid of sackless man.

Nought sair was Wully bashfu'. Wully spied
A pair of scissors at the lass's side;
Thar lowsed - he sleely droped the spinnel down
And what said Betty? Betty struive to frown;
Up flew her hand to souse the cowren lad:
But ah! I thought it fell not down owr sad.
What follow'd I think mickle to repeat:
My teeth aw watter'd then, and watter yet.

E'en weel is he 'at ever he was bworn!
He's free fraw aw this bitterment and scworn.
What mun I still be fashed wi' straglen sheep,
Wi' far fetched sighs, and things I said asleep;
Still shamefully left snaflen by my sel,
And still, still dog'd wi' the damn'd neame o' mell!

Whare's now the pith! (This luive! The deuce ga' wi't)
The pith I showed when eer we struive, to beat;
When a lang lwonin through the cworn I meade,
And bustlin far behind the leave survey'd.

Dear heart! That pith is geane and comes nae mair,
'Till Bitty's kindness sall the loss repair;
And she's not like (how should she?) to be kind,
Till I have freely spoken out my mind,
Till I have learnd to feace the maiden clean,
Oiled my slow tongue, and edged my sheepish een.

A buik theer is - a buik - the neame - shem faw't:
Some thing o' compliments I think they caw't:
'At meakes a clownish lad a clever spark,
O hed I this! This buik wa'd de my wark;

And I's resolved to hav'et what ever't cost:
My flute - for what's my flute if Betty's lost?
And if sae bonny a lass but be my bride,
I need not any comfort lait beside.

Farewell my flute then yet or Carlile fair;
When to the stationers I'll stright repair,
And bauldly for thur compliments enquear;
Care I a fardin, let the prentice jeer.

That duine - a handsome letter I'll indite,
Handsome as ever country lad did write;
A letter 'at sall tell her aw' I feel,
And aw my wants without a blush reveal.

But now the clouds brek off and sineways run;
Out frae his shelter lively luiks the sun,

Brave hearty blasts the droopin barley dry,
The lads are gawn to shear - and sae mun I.

***

Yes, yes, those drops may cool my outside heat,
Those cold blasts may wear the boiling sweat,
But my hot blood, my heart all in turmoil,
No cold blasts can wear, nor drops can cool.

Here, here it was (a road-light on the place),
The first time I got a glimpse of Betty's face:
Glad and distracted by this, the idiot fell, and there,
At the dale-head unluckily we shear:
Stupidly I grinned; nor could my eyes command,
'Till 'gash,' the sickle went into my hand.

The blood held in; the shearers all broke out
In peals of laughter; Betty looked about;
Red grew my fingers, redder by far my face:
What could I do in such a desperate case?

Away I ran; to grandma I moaned
My grandma (God be with her, now she's gone),
Skillfully stopped the gushing blood with cobwebs,
Then laid a healing plaster on the sore.
The healing plaster greatly eased the pain,
The scar indeed remains, but nothing more.

But not the other wound; the inward pain;
My grandma couldn't cure a bleeding heart;
I've borne the bitter torment three long years,
And must be forced to bear it all my life,
Unless Betty proves to be a kind physician,
For none but she has skill to medicine love.

But how should honest Betty give relief?
Betty's a perfect stranger to my grief.

I've often decided to explain my ailment [to her];
I've often decided, indeed, but all in vain.
A springing blush spread fast over either cheek,
Down Robin looked and not a word could speak.

Can I forget that night? (I never can!)
When on the clean-swept hearth the spindles ran;
The girls drew their line with busy speed,
The lads, as busy, minded every thread.
When, sad! Betty drew the line so slender
The thread went 'snap,' and down the spindle flew:

It made for me – the boys began to gape -
What could I do? I must, must pick it up;
I took it up and (which is the worst part of it)
Even reached it back without the sweet reward.

Oh lasting stain! Even now it's easy to trace;
A guilty conscience in my blushing face:
I would gladly wash it out but never can;
Still fair it stays like the blood of a spineless man.

Wully was not so bashful – Wully spied
A pair of scissors at the girl's side;
There freed, he fairly dropped the spindle down,
And what said Betty? Betty strove to frown;
Up flew her hand to smack the cowering boy,
But ah! I didn't think [her smack] was ill-received.
What followed I often think to repeat:
My teeth all watered then, and water still.

Still well is he that he was ever born!
He's free from all this bitterment and scorn.
Why should I still be bothered with shearing sheep,
With far-fetched sighs, and things I said asleep;
Still shamefully left pottering around by myself,
And still, still dogged with the damned name of mell!

Where's the pith now? (This love! The devil went with it!)
The pith I showed whenever we strove, to beat;

When I made a long lane through the corn,
And bustling far behind, surveyed the [???].

Dear heart! That pith is gone and comes no more,
'Till Betty's kindness shall repair the loss;
And she's not likely to be kind (how should she?)
'Till I have freely spoken out my mind.
'Till I have learned to face the girl straight-on,
Oiled my slow tongue, and edged my sheepish eyes.

A book there is - a book - the name - shame befall it!
Something of compliments I think they call it:
That makes a clownish boy a clever spark,
Oh, had I this, the book would do my work!

And I've resolved to have it, whatever the cost:
My flute - for what's my flute if Betty's lost?
And if so pretty a lass would be my bride,
I need not seek any further comfort.

Farewell my flute then, still, or Carlisle fair;
When to the stationers I'll straight repair;
And boldly ask for their compliments;
I don't care a farthing, let the prentice jeer.

With that done, I'll compose a handsome letter,
Handsome as any country boy did write;
A letter that shall tell her all I feel,
And reveal all my wants without revealing a blush.

But now the clouds break off and run into the past;
Out from his shelter lively looks the sun,
Brave hearty (wind) blasts the drooping barley dry,
The boys have gone to shear - and so must I.

***

The language of the poem is beautifully crafted. But setting aside aspects of the dialect which I have already investigated, can anything particular about Cumbrian culture in the early 18th century be taken from this poem, or is it simply an author familiar with the dialect using it to write what would otherwise be an ordinary love poem? I unfortunately lean towards the second of those; the subject matter is not uniquely English, let alone uniquely Cumbrian. Its interest comes from its heavily rural historical context, and the way the author expresses himself. The underlying feelings have probably been experienced, in some form, by most (if not all) people living in European-influenced countries, but we are allowed to experience them from the perspective of a young Cumbrian in the early 1700s. His contemplations about buying a book to help him express his words in writing (which implies that he is able to write and read); his likening of his tongue to an unoiled piece of equipment; his flashes of sympathy for Betty who, after all, is not really in a position to give relief to his struggle.

I have mentioned *Bobby Banks' Bodderment* several times, and will reproduce it here. I will not provide a translation this time, but will write what will probably end up being quite hefty footnotes to explain and discuss what needs explaining and discussing. The version I reproduce here can be found in *The Folk Speech of Cumberland and Some Districts Adjacent*, compiled in 1891 by Alexander Gibson.

Bobby Banks' Bodderment

She was ola's a top marketer was ooar Betty. She niver miss't gittin' t'best price gā'n beáth for butter an' eggs; an' she ken't hoo to bring t'ho'pennies heám[19]! Nūt like t'meást o' fellows' wives 'at thinks ther's néa hūrt i' warin' t' odd brass iv a pictur' beuk or gūd stūff for t' barnes, or m'appen sūm'at whyte as needless for the'rsels, - Betty ola's bring t'ho'pennies heám.

---

[19] 'She knew how to bring the ha'pennies home.'

Cockerm'uth's ooar reg'lar market - it's a gay bit t'bainer -- but
at t'time o' year when Kes'ick's full o' quality, ther's better
prices to be gitten theear; an' sooa o' through t'harvest time,
an' leater on, she ola's went to Kes'ick. Last back-end[20], hoover,
Betty was fash'd sadly wid rheumatics iv her back, an' yā week
she cud hardly git aboot at o', let alean gā to t'market. For a
while she wasn't mak ūp her mind whether to send me iv her
spot, or ooar eldest dowter, Faith; but as Faith was hardly
fowerteen - stiddy aneuf of her yeige, but rayder *yūng, - Betty*
thowte she'd better keep Faith at heám, an' let me tak'
t'marketin' to Kes'ick.

Of t'Setterda' mwornin', when it com', she hed us o' ūp an'
stūrrin', seúner nor sūm on us liket; an' when I'd gitten sūm'at
to eat, iv a hūgger mūgger mak' of a way, says Betty till me, says
she -

"Here's six an' twenty pūnd o' butter," says she.
"If thoo was gud for owte thoo wad git a shillin' a pūnd for't,
ivery slake. Here's five dozen of eggs," says she, "I wadn't give
a skell[21] o' them mair nor ten for sixpence," says she, "but thoo
mun git what thoo can," says she, "efter thu's fūnd oot what
ūdder fwoke's axin. When thu's meád thy market," says Betty,
"thu'll gā to t'draper's an' git mé a yard o' check for a brat[22], a
knot o' tape for strings tūl't, an' a hank o' threed to sowe't wid -
if I'd gud for nowte else, I can sowe yit," says she, wid a gurn;
"than thoo mūn git hoaf a pūnd o' tea an' a quarter of a steįn o'
suggar - they ken my price at Crosstet's - an' hoaf a steįn o'
soat, an' a pūnd o' seáp, an' hoaf a pūnd o' starch, an' a
penn'orth o' steán-blue, an' git mé a bottle o' that stuff to rūb
my back wid; an' than thoo ma' git two ounces o' 'bacca for

---

[20] 'Back-end' - Autumn. Still in use.

[21] 'Skell' - possibly the remnant of an unpalatalised form of 'shell,' or an Old Norse loan word from *skel.*

[22] Checked fabric for an apron. Possibly *Camperdoon*, a blue-and-white checked fabric popular in the area at the time.

thysel'.[23]

If thoo leúks hoaf as sharp as thoo sūd leúk, thu'll be through wid beáth thy marketin' an' thy shoppin' by twelve o'clock; an' thoo ma' gā an' git a bit o' dinner, like ūdder fwoke, at Mistress Boo's, an' a pint o' yall. Efter that t'seúner thoo starts for heám an' t'better. Noo thu'll mind an' forgit nowte? Ther' t'check, an' t'tape, an' t'threed, that's three things - t'tea, an' t'sugger, an' t'soat, an' t'seáp, an' t'starch, an' t'steán-blue, an' t'rūbbin' stuff, an' t'bacca - I's up-ho'd the' nūt to forgot that! - elebben. Ten things for me, an' yan for thysel. I think I've mejd o' plain aneuf; an' noo, if thoo misses owte I'll say thoo's a bigger clot-heid nor I've tejn the' for - an' that 'ill be sayin' néa lal!"

Many a fellow wad tak t'frunts if his wife spak till him i' that way. But bliss yé I've leev't lang aneśf wid Betty to know 'at it's no'but a way she hes o' shewin' her likin'. When she wants to be t'kindest an' best to yan, yan's ola's suer to git t'warst wūrd 'at she can finnd i' t'inside on her!

Well, I set off i' gūd fettle for Kes'ick, gat theear i' gradely time, an' pot ūp at Mistress Boo's. I hed a sharpish market, an' seún gat shot o'[24] my būtter an' eggs at better prices nor Betty toak't on. I bowte o' t'things 'at she wantit, an' t'bacca for mysel', an' gat a gud dinner at Mistress Boo's, an' a pint o' yall an' a crack.

He wad be a cliverish fellow 'at went ta Kes'ick an' gat oot on't adoot rain; an' suer aneúf, by t'time 'at I'd finished my pint an' my crack, it was cūmmin' doon as it knows hoo to cūm doon at Kes'ick.

But when it rains theear, they hev to deú as they deú ūnder Skiddaw, let it fo! An' wet or dry, I hed to git héam tull Betty.

---

[23] The full list in standard English: a yard of checked fabric, a knot of tape, a coil of thread, half a pound of tea, a quarter of a stone of sugar, half a stone of salt, a pound of soap, half a pound of starch, a penny's worth of stone-blue, a salve for her back, and two ounces of tobacco for himself.

[24] 'Gat shot o' - Got shot of, got rid of.

When I was aboot startin', I begon to think ther' was sum'at mair to tak wid me. I coontit t'things ower i' my basket hoaf a dozen times. Theear they o' warr - ten for Betty, yan for me! Than what the dang-ment was't I was forgittin? I was suer it was sūm'at, but for t'heart on me I cūdn't think what it med be. Efter considerin for a lang time, an' gittin' anūdder pint to help mé to consider, I set off i' t'rain wid my basket an' t'things in't, anonder my top-sark,[25] to keep o' dry.

Bee t'time I gat to Portinskeál, I'd begon to tire! T'wedder was slattery, t'rwoads was slashy, t'basket was heavy, an' t'top-sark meád me het; but t'thowtes o' hevin' forgitten sūm'at tew't mé t'warst of o'. I rūstit theear a bit - gat anudder pint, an' coontit my things ower and ower. "Ten for Betty! - yan for my-sel'." I cūd mak nowder mair nor less on them. Cockswūnters! - what hed I forgotten? Or what was't 'at meád mé suer I'd forgitten sūm'at when I'd o' t'things wid mé?

I teuk t'rwoad ageán mair nor hoaf crazy.

I stop't ūnder a tree aside Springbank, an' Dr. ------ com' ridin' up through t'rain, on his black galloway.

"Why, Robert," says he, "ye look as if ye'd lost something."[26]

"Nay, doctor," says I, "here t'check an' t'tape an t'threed - I' lost nowte, that's three.

Here t'soat, an' t'seáp, an' t'starch, an' t'steán-blue - that's sebben - I' lost nowte, but I' forgitten sum'at. Here t'tea, an t'sugger, an' t'rūbbin' bottle - that's ten; an' here t'bacca -

---

[25] He several times refers to his 'top-sark.' This may refer to a woolen outer layer elsewhere referred to as a *kytel* or *kirtel*, or it may just refer to an ordinary linen shirt, as opposed to an under-shirt. Intuition tells us that no sensible man would walk travel several miles in Cumbria without a thick outer layer, but then we are not necessarily dealing with a sensible man here. As he mentions holding the basket under the top-sark, it seems likely he is referring to a coat- or cloak-like garment.

[26] The doctor's speech is clearly differentiated from Bobby's; he may be southern, or he may simply speak less broadly, but he uses a number of standard English forms where Bobby does not.

*that's elebben. - Ten for Betty, an' yan for me! Ten for Betty, an'
yan for me!! Doctor, doctor," says I, "fwoke say ye ken o' things
- what hev I forgitten?"*

*"I'll tell ye what ye haven't forgotten," says he, "ye haven't
forgotten the ale at Keswick. Get home, Robert, get home," says
he, "and go to bed and sleep it off." I believe he thowte I was
drūnk, but I wasn't - I was no 'but maizelt wid tryin' to finnd oot
what I'd forgitten.*

*As I com nār to t'Swan wid two Necks[27] I fell in wid greet
Gweordie Howe, and says I, "Gweordie, my lad," says I, "I's
straddelt," says I, "I's fairly maiz't," says I, "I' left sūm'at ahint
me at Kes'ick, an' I've thowte aboot it till me heid's gā'n like a
job-jūrnal," says I, "an what it is I cannot tell."*

*"Can t'e nūt?" says Gweordie. "Can t'e nūt? Whey, than, cūm
in an' see if a pint o' yall'll help thé'."[28]*

*Well, I steud[29] pints, an' Gweordie steud pints, an' I steud pints
ageán. Anūdder time I wad ha' been thinkin' aboot what Betty
wad say till o' this pintin', but I was gittin' despert aboot what
I'd forgitten at Kes'ick, an' I cūd think o' nowte else.*

*T'yall was gud aneúf, but it dúdn't kest a morsel o' leet on what
was bodderin' on ma sa sair, an' I teuk t'rwoad ageán finndin'
as if I was farder off't nor iver.*

*T'rain keep't cūmmin' doon - t'rwoad gat softer an' softer -
t'basket gat heavier an' heavier - t'top sark hetter an' hetter, an'
my heid queerer an' queerer.[30] If I stopt anonder ya tree i'
t'wūd, I stopt anonder twenty, an' coontit ower t'things i'
t'basket till they begon to shap' theirsels intil i' mak's o' barnish
sangs i' my heid, and I fūnd mysel' creunin' away at sec bits of
rhymes as thūr -*

---

[27] The 'Swan with Two Necks' is presumably a public house.

[28] Gweordie also speaks slightly differently, if only in his
pronunciation of 'why' as 'whey,' suggesting a north-eastern
Cumbrian accent.

[29] The word *steud* ('stood') is used humourously to imply that
drinking pints was an ordeal for them.

[30] 'Queer' here means 'drunk.' Elsewhere it means 'unusual.'

Ten things an' yan, Bobby,
Ten things an' yan;
Here five an' five for Betty Banks,
An' yan for Betty's man.

"Lord presarve oor wits - sec as they ūrr," says I.
"I mūn be gā'n wrang i' my heid when I've teán till mackin'
sangs!" But t'queerest break was 'at I dūddn't mak' them - they
meád thersel's - an' they meád me sing them an' o', whether I
wad or nūt - an' off I went ageán till a different teún -

Says Betty - says she; says Betty till me -
"If owte thoo contrives to forgit,
I'll reckon thé daizter an' dafter," says she,
"Nor iver I've reckon't thé yit."
I's daizter an' dafter nor iver, she'll say,
An' marry, she willn't say wrang!
But scoald as she will, ey, an' gūrn as she may,
I'll sing her a bonnie lāl sang, lāl sang,
I'll sing her a bonnie lāl sang.

"Well! It hes cūm't till whoa wad hae thowte it," says I, "if I
cannot stop mysel' frae mackin' sangs an' singin' them of a wet
day i' Widdup Wūd. I'll coont t'things ower ageán," says I, "an'
see if that'll stop ma." Ye ma' believe ma or nūt, as ye like, but
iv anūdder tick-tack theer was I coontin' t'things ower iv a sang:

Here t'check an' t'tape an' t'threed, oald lad!
Here t'soat an' t'sugger an' t'tea -
Seáp, starch, steán-blue, an' t'bottle to rub,
An' t'bacca by 'tsel' on't for me,
Here t'bacca by 'tsel' on't for me, me, me,
Here t'bacca by 'tsel' on't for me.
I'll niver git heám while Bobby's my neám,
But maffle an' sing till I dee, dee, dee,

But maffle an' sing till I dee.

"Weel, weel," says I, "if I is oot o' my senses - I is oot o' my senses, an' that's o' aboot it." - But

> *Loavins what'll Betty think, Betty think, Betty think,*
> *Loavins what'll Betty think if Bobby bide away?*
> *She'll sweer he's warin' t'brass i' drink, t'brass i'*
> *drink, t'brass i' drink,*
> *She'll sweet he's warin' t'brass i' drink this varra*
> *market-day.*
> *She's thrimlin' for her būtter-brass, but willn't thrimle*
> *lang.*
> *For Bobby lad, thū's hūr to feáce, thū's hūr to feáce,*
> *thū's hūr to feáce,[31]*
> *For Bobby lad, thū's hūr to feáce; she'll m'appen*
> *change thy sang.*

Sang or néa sang, t'thowtes o' hevin "hūr to feáce," an' that gaily séun, rayder brong me to my oan oald sel' ageán. I set off yance mair, an' this time, I dūdn't stop while I gat fairly into t'foald.
Faith seed me cūmmin', an' met me ootside o' t'hoose dooar, an' says Faith, "Whoar t'meear an' t'car, fadder?" I dropp't my basket, an' I geápt at her! Lal Jacop com runnin' oot, an' says Jacop,
"Fadder, whoar t'meear an' t'car?[32]" I swattit mysel' doon on t'steán binch, an' I glower't at them - first at yan an' than at t'udder on them. Betty com limpin' by t'God-speed, an' says Betty,
"What hes t'e meád o' t'car an' t'meear, thoo maizlin'?"

---

[31] Here, the author rhymes *feáce* ('face') with *brass* ('money'), suggesting that he pronounces this word, and presumably others in its lexical set, with /jɐ/ rather than a centering diphthong.
[32] "Where are the mare and cart?"

I gat my speech ageán when Betty spak', an', hoaf crazet an'
hoaf cryin', I shootit oot,
"Od's wūns an' deeth, that's what I' forgitten!"
That was what I said. What Betty said I think I willn't tell yé.

***

In terms of actual pronunciation, little is to be gleaned here - the author uses diacritics (marks above letters) in an almost random way, possibly just to make the text seem more foreign to a southern reader, and uses apostrophes a bit overzealously. Having said that, I have included this story mostly because I really enjoy it. It builds up to its punchline very effectively; it starts with Betty laying out the things Bobby must buy, and we are led to expect that he will forget one of them. He gets to Keswick and does better than expected at the market, but on his way home, he feels he has forgotten something. Our attention is expertly kept attached to the list of things he was told to buy; it doesn't occur to us, or at least it didn't occur to me, that he might have forgotten the horse and cart. Betty's full wrath is then brought upon Bobby, who is painted as a man living in fear of his wife, but respecting her authority on market matters.

On another topic: the Herdwick is not the only breed of sheep suited for fell grazing. Although it is the staple breed of the fells, the lesser-known Rough Fell is also kept, particularly in the southern part of Cumbria. They are larger than Herdwicks, having a pale yellowish-white fleece and a black face, aside from the area around its nose and mouth, which is white. Both *tups* ('rams') and *yows* ('ewes') have tightly-coiled horns. This is another point of contrast to Herdwicks, among which *tups* are generally horned, and *yows* polled[33].

The third breed of sheep grazed on the fells is the Swaledale, or *Swadal* /ˈswɛːdl/ in broad Cumbrian. They are named for a

---

[33] Selectively bred not to have horns.

valley in Yorkshire and are similar in colouration to the Rough Fell, to which they are probably related. The key difference is that Swaledales have white areas around the eyes. Both males and females are horned, but males' horns are markedly larger. All three breeds must be kept and maintained in their own particular way, although there are obviously commonalities. For an actual fell-farmer's breakdown, I would highly recommend James Rebanks' *The Illustrated Herdwick Shepherd*, as well as *The Shepherd's Life* by the same author, but by way of summary, and in the knowledge that I will probably get the timings a bit off: towards the end of December, *yows* are loosed onto the fell. Because they are *heftit,* they tend not to stray far from the bit of fell they are attached to; there is no need to enclose them. The few ewes that stray too far end up collected by neighbouring farmers and returned to their owners at regular shepherd's meets. In Spring, they are gathered to lamb in enclosed lang in the bottom of the valley (this way, the shepherd can keep an eye on them and help them if needed), and are then loosed onto the fell with their lambs (unless they have twin lambs, in which case they are kept on lower ground, where they can be kept an eye on). Whilst on the fell with their mothers, lambs develop their *hefting* instinct. In early summer, the sheep are gathered from the fell and *clipped* ('sheared'). By mid-Autumn, lambs are weaned so that they no longer rely on their mothers, and fit *yows* are returned to the fell. Unfit or elderly *yows* are taken 'out of circulation,' as it were, and either kept closer to home for breeding with tups to produce crossbreeds, or sold to other farms. Shortly afterwards, *wedders* ('castrated male lambs') are sold to lowland farmers and will not return to the fell. Towards the start of winter, *gimmers* (females born the previous spring) are sent to spend winter on lowland farms, where they can be better fed and sustained. These are the same lambs that will return in spring. At the same time, breeding *tups* and *yows* are loosed in the bottom of the valley to mingle with each other. Excepting details like the invention of the quad bike, fell-farming has been practiced continuously in this way for centuries, and has come up against numerous attempts to change it beyond recognition or stop it all together, often in the interest of 'agricultural improvement.' The end of fell-farming has been predicted numerous times over the last four hundred years and has never occurred, and I put this down to two things. Firstly, the fells are not much good for anything else (particularly nothing agricultural). Secondly, to be a Cumbrian fell-farmer is to be a member of a cultural group rooted in a very specific kind of animal husbandry. To stop practicing fell-farming is not the equivalent of changing jobs - to stop practicing fell-farming is to discard the lens through which the fell-farmer sees everything else in his or her life. On a broader scale, archaic and sustainable traditions of animal husbandry took centuries to form, and cannot be quickly re-invented if they disappear. They rely on generational knowledge that does not exist in any book.

Terry McCormick's book *Lake District Fell Farming* talks in more detail about the historical struggles of fell-farmers against pre-industrial-revolution agricultural 'improvement,' and the ways in which shepherds have had to adapt in order to stay afloat, as well as giving a detailed account of the environmental problems, such as livestock disease outbreaks (the most recent major one of which was, of course, the foot and mouth pandemic of 2001) and severe winters.

Sheep-farming has not historically been the only primary occupation of Cumbrians. Lowland farming was, and is, extensively carried out. Gamekeeping is also vital to the upkeep of the local moorland environment; swathes of Cumbrian upland are covered in heather moors inhabited by grouse and hares. The heather must be burnt in a controlled way in order to promote new growth, and to mitigate the possibility of larger, uncontrollable fires.

Cumbrians in urban areas, particularly along the western coast, were involved in coal mining from the industrial revolution until the 1980s, and a local culture (which I unfortunately know too little about to confidently describe) has built up around this.

Before I address folklore, I will address smaller aspects of everyday life that do not fall into that category. William Dickinson has included several of them in his 1878-9 *Glossary*.

It was known for young boys to steal sheaves of peas and burn them publicly, and for all of the local boys to sift through the ashes and embers looking for peas that were scorched but still intact.

Dickinson's glossary, through providing local vocabulary, also lets us in on some of the mundane artefacts people used. A *cannelbark* was a small bark box for holding candles. The candles were lit with *bunnels* (c.f English *bundles*), dried stems of the cow parsnip. When transporting blocks of butter, they were wrapped in mountain dock leaves before being placed in a basket. In the 18th century, *clog wheels* - large spokeless wheels, made from thick planks of wood – were used on carts. A hefty *clout nail* would be used to attach the iron hoop to the wheel. *Coom cards* are the coarsest cards in the sequence when carding wool.

A *cowp* is a small cart used for traversing fellsides. This is related to the verb *cowp* (to exchange). The origin is the old Norse *kaupa* (to buy). Standard English has a cognate derived from the Old English word; *cheap* (as in 'inexpensive'). The Cumbrian and standard English cognates both relate to barter and exchange, but the Cumbrian one is closer to the earlier meaning. Another cognate is the German *kaufen* (to buy). From the verb *cowp* are derived two other terms: *cowper hand* (the upper hand (e.g. in a sales negotiation)), and *cowper word* (the first word in a negotiation or argument; whoever says the *cowper word* has the advantage).

A *cwose huus* is a house with a dead person in it. *Cronk* is the sound made by a raven (similar to the Icelandic equivalent, *krunk*). It was customary to place the spoon across the cup when one finished drinking tea. An *egbattle* was a person who incited others to fight or argue (related to the term *to egg on*). When playing 'blind man's buff,' children would sing the following song as they spun the person around;

> *"Antony blindman kens ta me,*
> *Sen I bought butter and cheese o' thee?*
> *I ga' the my pot, I ga' the my pan,*
> *I ga' the o' I hed but a rap ho'penny*

I gave a poor oald man."

On that note, as well as a number of stories, 19th-century literature treats us to several Cumbrian *sangs* ('songs; ballads'). The best collection, and probably the oldest, is by Robert Anderson, and was written around the turn of the 19th century. Most of the songs have the tune of a better-known folk song written at the top, suggesting melodies were recycled and re-used. As with other traditional English folk music spanning the second millennium, it seems to have been mostly in quadruple or triple meter, and very often included repetition of a particular refrain consisting of one or several lines. These refrains could be actual words, or nonsense sounds, as in *The Worton Wedding*:

> *Whurry-whum, Whuddle-whum!*
> *Whulty-whalty, wha wha wha!*
> *An derry-dum, deedle-dum!*
> *Derry-ey den-dee!*

Later shepherds meets, which still occur today, seem to have had communal singing as a core element, although that does not preclude people singing to each other in smaller-scale social environments, or to themselves while they worked or travelled[34] (both being valid cultural expressions in themselves).

---

[34] *Bobby Brown's Bodderment* describes the focal character making up and singing songs to himself as he goes home, to help him remember what he needed to buy.

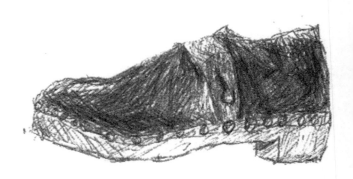

Cumbrian Folklore.

The folklore of Cumbria is closely tied to that of the rest of rural northern England. The most prominent and well-described pieces of folklore are to be found in 19th-century volumes, although broader northern trends can be found in folklore compendiums. As any rich culture of superstitions does, rural English folklore attributed more agency to natural processes than Euroamerican science might.

A few aspects of the lore, particularly those related to creatures of the countryside and household, might hark back to a broader northwestern European tradition. The words used to describe these creatures are often annoyingly vague, which could also be said of equivalent words in Old English such as *ælf, eoten* and *dweorg*, which I dare not even give translations for without a lengthy diversion explaining the possible interpretations of them. I have found, leafing through (mostly Victorian) literature on the subject, that these writers have a keen interest in what they perceive to be the paranormal. It's this interest, after all, that has driven them to write the books. This interest means that a lot of occultist ideas, which were in vogue at the time, permeate the works, and the descriptions of the folklore end up being very influenced by these ideas. Whether the average rural person would have identified with those aspects of the lore is questionable. I am sure that my own biases will play into this chapter, but I will try to avoid this as best I can.

We cannot know how people 200 or 400 years ago saw the world. We can make some suggestions: for example, it seems likely that people largely saw folklore and superstition as part of their everyday lives, distinct from their religion. It seems like folklore may have affected their everyday undertakings in small ways; certain stories call for a horseshoe or a bowl of salt to be left by the doorstep to keep away certain things.

Brownies, hobs or *dobbies* were little men who inhabited particular households and rarely or never allowed themselves to be seen. They are supposed to have sometimes helped the homeowner in their daily tasks, gathering hay or tidying up.

Some were thought to live in a specific place in the house or garden. The *hob* would accept small gifts of food. However, if it were ever left a gift of clothing, it would become upset. Of course, given its tendency to avoid people, it would only find the gift when there was nobody in the room. On finding the gift, it could apparently be heard to say a rhyme. The exact wording of the rhyme varies. William Henderson, writing in 1879, gives no examples from northern England, but three from Scotland. Bear in mind the language may have been anglicized slightly.

> *A new mantle and a new hood,*
> *Poor brownie! Ye'll ne'er do mair good.*

> *Gie brownie coat, gie brownie sark,*
> *Ye's get nea mair o brownie's wark.*

> *Red breeks and a ruffled sark!*
> *Ye'll no get me to do yer wark!*

Very, very close parallels to this idea exist not only in south-western England, but also in Germany. In the former case, pixies (or *piskies*), if given a new article of clothing, will shout something like;

> *Piskie fine, piskie gay,*
> *Piskie now will run away.*

Of the latter case, the story of the Elves and the Shoemaker is illustrative. It's a story we all vaguely know, but it has many close parallels to the northern English stories of *hobs* and *dobbies*; it describes an impoverished shoemaker discovering that three elves have been making high-quality shoes for him to sell. The ending depends on the variant of the story, but in the version published by the brothers Grimm, the shoemaker and his wife leave the elves a set of clothes to thank them for their work, and hear the elves (*Wichtelmänner*) sing this rhyme;

Sind wir nicht Knaben glatt und fein?
Was soll'n wir länger Schuster sein?

Are we not sleek and fine boys?
Why should we be shoemakers any longer?

And then they disappear. In the original German, the name of the story is *Die Wichtelmänner* (the gnome-men). In the Netherlands, the equivalent creature is the *kabouter*. It is clearly a tradition that spans northwestern European cultures, then. The Scandinavian *nisse* and *tomte,* both household spirits almost perfectly matching the German and northern English descriptions, show that the concept is not absent in northern European cultures, either. Cross-culturally, these things are often said to wear conical red hats (sometimes in Scotland actually being referred to as *redcaps*). The part about them happily receiving small gifts of food seems to be near-universal to the concept. So is the point about them running away if given clothes. Their motivation here is not always obvious. In the German story, it seems as though they take the clothes and decide that they look nice in them, and do not need to spend their time fixing shoes anymore. In the English and Scottish stories, you could interpret the rhymes in a number of ways; they may be similar in motivation to the German elves, or they may become offended by the gift and refuse to do any more work. Alternatively, they may be somehow bound to do the work up until the point that they are given clothes.

That these stories exist in insular areas of Germanic influence, as well as on the continent, suggests to me that they stem from an older tradition, which might go back to Proto-Germanic. It certainly doesn't seem ridiculous to suggest that these things were believed in during the Anglo-Saxon period; the ritual aspects of Christian and pre-Christian religion, both on the continent and in England, are so scarcely written about, that a lack of writing about common superstitions isn't out-of-place at all. They would have seen them as trivial, and so universally-recognised that they might not have seen any point in putting them to paper. It would be like a modern author writing a text on how to use a knife and fork.

But if the Anglo-Saxons believed in these things, did they refer to them as *ælfe* ('elves')? The modern word *elf*, which it would not be inappropriate to apply to a *hob* or *dobby*, does not necessarily have the same connotations as the Anglo-Saxon word. The Anglo-Saxon word for a *hob* may just never have been written down. What seems most likely to me is that the Anglo-Saxon vocabulary on the subject worked similarly to the later northern English vocabulary on the subject. That is, there were a few words in circulation, and a few concepts in circulation, and exactly which word applied to which concept differed from region to region, or from story to story.

Dobby is of uncertain etymology. For all we know, it might have an unattested Old English root; something like **dobig*. However, *hob* seems to have been an old nickname for people called Robert. Remember that some English nicknames are not exact contractions of the original name; 'Bill' can be short for 'William,' and 'Dick' can be short for 'Richard.'

Various points of comparison could be drawn between the boggarts of north-western English folklore and the *eotenas* referenced by the Anglo Saxons. *Eoten* has long been translated as *giant*, but this seems inappropriate. They are never described as being especially large in relation to anything else. In fact, they are rarely described in terms of their physical attributes at all. Grendel and his mother are described as *eotenas* a number of times. A sword is described as *eotenisc* ('eotenish'). Beyond that, there is some discussion of Grendel in terms of what sorts of places he inhabits;

> *Wæs se grimma gaest Grendel hatan*
> *Maere mearcstapa se þe moras heold*
> *Fen ond fæsten, fifelcynnes heard.*

> The terrible beast was called Grendel,
> Infamous walker of the boundaries, who held the moors,
> Fen and fortress, the swamp-monsters' dwelling.

The idea is clearly one of uninhabited and distant places; the sorts of places that one might cross on one's way to somewhere else, but not the sort of place a person would live. Many descriptions of boggarts paint a similar picture - although they are more likely to live near places that humans inhabit. A boggart is likely to be associated with a particular spot; a particular tree, wall, field, marsh or other such place.

Paradoxically, one thing that ties *eotenas* to boggarts is how poor an idea the literature gives about them. J.K. Rowling presumably played upon this in her representation of boggarts in the *Harry Potter* series; she describes them as changing shape according to what the person encountering them is most afraid of. In folklore, there *are* physical descriptions of them, but it is rare to see two descriptions that match; it seems as though local ideas about their appearance came and went, and still come and go in pockets where they are still believed in.

The word *boggart* would be the equivalent to a standard English **boggard* (compare *braggard* and *dotard*), with the final *-t* a result of the devoicing of many instances of unstressed word-final /d/, as I have discussed earlier. The *bogg-* part makes numerous appearances across northern folklore, being present in *boggle* as well. *Bugbear* and *boman* may also be related. It seems most likely, and is assumed by many writers, that *bogg-* is cognate with English *bug*, with the more general sense of 'an unpleasant creature.'

One commonality across several boggart stories is that you are not supposed to name them. Whether this means that a given boggart has a specific name that you are not meant to say, or that you should not say the word 'boggart' at all, I'm not sure - but if there is any connection between boggarts and *eotenas*, the lack of continuity in the name of the creature might be put down to a taboo about naming it. The later Cumbrian reflex of *eoten* would be something like **yutn* (cf. *eode - yud*; *eow - yow*). I'm not aware of any word bearing this relation. The idea of a taboo relating to the 'true name' of something would certainly not be unique to Cumbrian.

Reading about stories which contain such ambiguity leads us to try to make up for it by transposing our own spiritual views onto them; we may feel that certain stories resonate with us in particular ways. For example, a fan of *The Lord of the Rings* might read *Beowulf* and it might trigger a similar emotional response; excitement, escapism, mystery, or whatever else. Somebody who is interested in neopagan movements might read into things in their own particular way, as well. Anybody's reading of a story or tradition is valid, but it is probably not correct to say that the people who originally held these beliefs would have seen them in the same way that a modern person does.

This is why I have tried to avoid words like *sprite, goblin, wight* and so on; they have been extensively used by modern fantasy writers, and so to use them is to drag the connotations of these old stories in various directions. There are people in rural Lancashire, for example, who still believe that the influence of witches affects their lives – not because they have read it in a book, but because they were taught it by their parents, who were in turn taught it by their parents.

The insult *oaf* is one of the few commonly-understood words that I would put down as a loan word *from* Cumbrian *to* standard English; it is cognate with *elf*, and has exactly the phonological development we would expect from Anglian Old English *alf*. Around the time of the great vowel shift, the /l/ was deleted and the vowel lengthened, leaving **aaf*. According to the same change that produced *o', wo', fo'* (all, wall, fall), the word became *oaf*. The original implication of *oaf* seems to have been similar to the concept of a changeling; the idea that a person was replaced with an elf at birth, and behaves in a stupid or unusual way as a result.

Creatures are not the only subjects of folklore; general superstitions are also of keen interest. In this vein, more examples can be found that are specific to Cumberland and Westmorland, but I will start with one known across the whole of England; the idea that, if a child is born at a specific time, they will grow up to be unusually perceptive. They will know in advance if somebody close to them is going to die, and they may be able to see ghosts. A Cumbrian twist on this is the idea of a *swarth*.

A *swarth* is the image of somebody that appears shortly before or shortly after they die. It is supposed to be indistinguishable from the living person; there are no strange lights or anything traditionally associated with a ghost. Henderson (1879) lists several stories he has gathered about swarths and related ideas in other northern counties, saying that they do not usually talk. Relatives of mine have talked about similar things, claiming that they *do* talk sometimes, but generally do not mean harm. They might be seen wandering a path, making a cup of tea, reading a book. They might walk into the room, say something and then leave. The word *swarth* comes from the Old English *sweart* ('black'), and is related to standard English *swarthy*.

This superstition seems to be related to the idea that certain people have a deeper intuition than others, being able to tell when others are going to die or when something unpleasant is going to happen. My own grandmother, and other people I know and have spoken to, have had experiences with these sorts of things, and these sorts of beliefs are certainly not restricted to Cumbria, being widespread in northern England. It is borne of a kind of spirituality that I find myself drawn to, having been occasionally privy to stories of it as a child.

A *boggle* or *bogle* is a much broader term, describing any kind of ghost or apparition. Stories about *boggles* may be humorous; in *Crossyat's Boggle*, a drunk man is walking home at night and is attacked by what he thinks is a ghost, but what turns out to be an owl. Some stories are more serious in tone, but tend just to describe encounters; there is rarely an explanation given for what the thing is or why it is there.

A *barghest* - of uncertain etymology, but apparently pronounced something like /ˈbɜːrgest/ - is another creature whose description varies from story to story. A tradition found in several northern English counties holds that the *barghest* is a black dog associated with death; when a person is going to die, it comes and lies across their doorstep. During a person's funeral, this black dog was supposed to lead all of the other dogs in the village in a great funeral procession, striking anybody with its paw if they got in its way. It was supposed to be unable to cross rivers, and was local to particular areas. The word *barghest* could also be used quite interchangeably with *boggart*.

To speak of some other traditional knowledge - Henderson says that it is an old Cumberland belief that whichever way a bull faces as he sleeps on Halloween night, that is the direction the wind will blow from during the winter. Most traditions relating to Halloween, however, seem to have fizzled out by the mid 20th century, and the celebration (or even acknowledgement) of it has reappeared very recently on account of American influence. I will now provide two readings relating to folklore. The first is a more humorous story; the second is more serious. Again, the first text is from an 1891 book by Alexander Gibson.

Branthet Neuk Boggle

'At Marron beck's a bonnie beck, what mazelin wad deny?
An' what compares wi' Branthet Néuk[35] that Marron beck ga's by?
Wid hooses white, an' worchets green, an' Marron runnin' clear,
Eigh! Branthet Néuk's a heartsome spot i' t'sunny time o' year!

But loave! It is a dowly pléace when winter neets growe lang;
For t'lwoan ligs dark atween its banks, a flaysome rwoad to gang
When t'wind rwoars wild in t'trees aboon, an' Marron rwoars below,

---

[35] *Neuk* has a broader meaning than its English cognate 'nook,' also meaning 'corner' or 'dwelling.'

An' Branthet Néuk's a hantit spot, as I've some reeght[36] to know.

They say a heidless woman woaks at sartin neeghts o' t' year,
An' gréans an' yewls at sek a rate as freeghtens fwoke to hear;
I wadn't mind sek téals, but yance I gat a freeght me-sel,
I' Branthet Neuk, an' hoo it was, just lissen an' I'll tell.

Ya neeght, lang sen, at Kersmas time, wid Kersmas mak o'
wedder,
A lock on us at Branthet met, to hev a glass togidder,[37]
We crack't, an' jwok't, an' drank, an' smeuk't, while hoaf o' t'
neeght went by,
For Isbel Simon drink was gud, an' we were rayder dry!

T'was lownd an' léat - past yan o'clock - wid nut a spark o'
moon:
An' like a clood o' cardit woo, thick snow keep't sinkin' doon,
When reeght up t'néuk, three Jwohns an' me went wadin' héam
through t'snow,
Jwohn Suntan, an' Jwohn Bell o' t' rayes, an' Jwohn o'
Craypless ho.

We'd gitten hoaf o' t' way up t' lwoan, nar Edard Beeby yat,
An' theear we stop't, for marcy me! A parlish freeght we gat,
Lood gréans we heard - lang hollow beels - 'at shak't oor varra
béans,
"For God-séak, lads, mak on," sez yan, "Them t'heidless
woman' gréans!"

---

[36] The author chooses to spell words in the *night* set with a *gh* digraph. This probably does not reflect an actual sound, as no other 19th-century author mentions it as still existing, although Dickinson remarks that it existed 'within memory.'

[37] *Wedder* ('weather') and *togidder* ('together') are in a rhyming couplet with each other, but the author chooses to spell them with different letters, suggesting a merger or near-merger.

"But nay," sez I, "If wantin' t' heid, she raises sek a rout,
I'd like to see what way she taks to fetch sek haybays oot,
They say yan stops a woman's noise when yan taks off her heid,
But this, by gock! Wad mak yan sweer they're noisy whick or
deid."

Its Burns 'at says Jwohn Barleycworn can mak yan bold as
brass;[38]
An' Isbel drink méad me quite keen this gréanin' thing to féace.
We shootit Edard Beeby up, an' méad him git a leeght,
He grummel't sair to be disturb't at sek a time o' neeght,

But brong yan oot, an', led bee t'lugs, we follow't efter t' soond,
While clwose to t' swine-hull dooar we com, an' stopt, an'
gedder't roond,
"By gockers[39], lads!" Jwohn Suntan said, "It's no 'but Edard
Swine!"
"Nay, nay," sez Edard, "mine's i' soat - it's néa pig o' mine."

"Well, I'll ga in, an' see," sez I. O' t' rest steud leukin on
As in I creep't wid t' leeght an' fund greit lang Joe Nicholson
Hoaf cover't up wid mucky strea - soond asleep - an' snworin,
As if o' t' bulls o' Dean were theear, an' ivery bull was rwoarin.

We trail't him oot, an' prop't him up agéan t'oald swine-hull
wo',
And daze't wid coald he glower't aboot, an' daddert like a fo',
We help't 'im in, an' hap't 'im weel, on t'squab aback o' t'
dooar,
He said his wife hed barr't 'im oot, as oft she'd deun afooar.

Says Jwohn o' t' rayes, "If iv'ry neeght he maks sa gurt a din,

---

[38] A reference to an old folk song. 'John Barleycorn' is a
personification of grain alcohols such as beer and whisky.
[39] A minced oath meaning 'by God.'

174

It's rayder queer a wife like his sud iver let him in;
It's varra weel we hard him though, he med ha' deet o' coald!
Come, let's git héam! - an' laughin loud, we lonter't oot o' t'
foald.

Jwohn Suntan's rwoad left oor's gay seun, an' sooa[40] dud Jwohn
Bell's,
An' Jwohn o' Craypless ho' an' me went poapin on oorsels,
An' no'but slow, for t'snow was thick, an' méad it bad to woke,
Sooa mid-leg deep we striddel't on, but offen steud to toke.

Jwohn hed a faymish crack in 'im - his fadder hed afooar 'im -
At téals an' sangs, an' sec like fun nut many cud cum ower 'im,
An' theear an' than, dud Jwohn set on, at t'furst gud rist we
téuk,
To tell me hoo ther' com to be a ghost i' Branthet Néuk.

Sez Jwohn, sez he, "I' Branthet Néuk, as varra weel thoo knows,
'Tween t'beck an' Edard Beeby' hoose ther' stands some
brocken wo's;
Lang sen, when they hed roofs on them, yance, léatish on i'
t'year,
Some tinkley fwoke gat leave fray t'lword, an' com to winter
theear.

"Two oald fwoke, wid a scrowe o' barns, an' ya son, just a man
-
A handy chap to shap a speun, or cloot a pot or pan -
An' this chap hed a bonnie wife, 'at dudn't leuk like t'rest,
But fair, clean-skinn't, an' léady-like, an' ol'as nicely drest.

"An' hoo she com to be wid them was niver reeghtly known,

---

[40] Several times, the author extends what would normally be single-syllable words to two syllables where they contain diphthongs. This may reflect a particular variety, but is more likely to be a stylistic choice.

But nebbers so' she wasn't used as if she'd been the'r oan;
For t'oald fwoke soas't her neet an' day, - her man - a durty tike!
Wad bray her wid a besom-stick, a thyvel, or sec like;

"Tull yance a nebber téuk her in, when t'tinklers flang her oot,
An' she let fo' a wurd or two 'at bring a change aboot;
She telt o' sum stown cheese an' sheep, an' whoar they hed them hidden;
Of mutton up on t'sleeping loft, an' skins anonder t'midden.

"It wasn't many wurds she said - but wurds she said anew
To bring t'oald tinkler an' her man tull what was weel the'r due;
For lang i' Carel jail they laid, an' when t'assize com on,
T'judge let t'oald waistrel lowce agéan, but hang't his whopeful son.

"An' back frae Carel t'tinkler com, to Branthet reeght away,
An' 'ticet t'pooar lass frae t'nebber's hoose whoar she'd been fain to stay;
He promish't fair to treat her weel, an' dud while t'seckint neeght,
An' than (reeght pleas't was Branthet fwok) he méad a moonleeght fleeght.

"An' days went by an' néabody went nar to t'tinkler's dooar,
At last some barnes peep't in an' so' some huller't bléud on t'flooar,
An' than t'hoose dooar was druven in, an' sec a seeght was theer,
'At sum 'at so't went reid wid réage, an' sum went white wid fear.

"Squeez't up intull a durty néuk, an' bléady, stark an' deid,
They fund that nice young lass's corp, bit niver fund her heid;
T'oald tinkler hound hed hagg't it off afooar he méad a fleeght on't,

An' téan it wid 'im, fwoke suppwos't, to gud his-sel' wid t'seet
on't.

"An nin o' t'clan at efter that i' t'country side was seen.
But iver sen a hantit spot hes that Néuk-lonning been,
For t'murder't woman wokes aboot, an' gréans, for o' she's
deid,
As lood as what we hard to neeght - they say she laits her heid!"

"Wey, weel déun, Jwohn!" to Jwohn sez I, "an' thanks ta for thy
téal,
It's méad me hoaf forgit hoo t'snow maks o' my teéas géal;
Thu's just at héam - gud neeght, my lad, but furst hear this fray
me,
If iv'ry téal 'at's telt be true, thy stwory's néa lee!"

***

This is a comedic account of the walk home after a night spent
drinking, something I'm sure many of us have our own
experiences of. The ghost in particular is not especially
Cumbrian or northern English in nature; it does not match the
description of a *swarth*, instead being a fairly ordinary ghost
story that happens to be set in Cumbria. Whether there is any
local reality to the story is not clear.

The story does not so much have a punchline as a moment of
light relief at the end; after the story told by the character of
Jwohn, the author comments, 'If every tale that's told is true,
your story's no lie!'

Of Gibson's assorted stories, perhaps the most interesting sample
of Cumbrian folklore in the late 19th century is found in *Oxenfell
Dobby*. This story is told from the perspective of a non-
Cumbrian writing mostly in standard English, and so there is
little sense in me reproducing it here, but it describes his
conversations with a Cumbrian man who accompanies him
through the landscape of a snowy winter night. He describes the

Cumbrian man as riding a 'rough, clumsy little' horse. The man is guiding him to his farm.

At a particular point in the journey, the Cumbrian man suggests that they take a rougher, longer path rather than the smoother and more direct one. The narrator protests, but his guide insists, saying that nobody local would hire him to travel that road, and that he would explain why when they were safely by his fireside. The narrator asks if there is a story, to which he replies:

> *It's nowte mitch of a stooary, bit what ther's on't 's true,*
> *an' that's meear ner can be said for many a better stooary.*

> It's not much of a story, but what there is of it is true, and
> that's more than can be said for many a better story.

At the fireside, the man goes into more detail, explaining that ten years prior, he had been out hunting hares on a similarly snowy night. It is heavily implied he did not want to be seen transporting the hares he had caught, having done so illegally. On the road at Oxenfell - the one he had advised the narrator not to take - he heard a few men talking some way in front of him, but was unable to see them because of the topography of the land and the surrounding walls.

The guide, not wanting to be caught with his poached hares, climbed over a drystone wall into a field, sitting with his back against the wall to let the men pass. As they approached, their speech became more heated until they were shouting at each other aggressively, and then one man let out a loud scream. Jumping back over the wall to ensure nobody was injured, the guide saw that there was nobody there. Not only was there nobody there, but there were no footprints in the snow other than his own -

> *An' now I've telt ye t'reason 'at I wodn't cu' heeam by*
> *Oxenfell Cross. I niver hev been, 'cept i' dayleet, on*
> *t'rooad whar them fellows woaks, an' I niver will, sa lang*
> *as I can git anudder 'at's less nor a scooar o' miles about.*

And now I've told you the reason that I wouldn't come home by Oxenfell Cross. I never have been, except in daylight, on the road where those fellows walk, and I never will, as long as I can use another that's less than twenty miles longer.

The man goes on to explain that the 'Oxenfell Dobby' has been seen - or encountered, at least - by hundreds of people, and that there is a local story that explains how it has come to be there. A Scottish gardener, apparently, had moved to the nearby village of Rydal Hall. He had taken a liking to a woman called Betty[41]. Betty had been the 'sweetheart' of a man named Jack Slipe, but as soon as this Scotch gardener arrived, she began seeing him instead.

One night, this gardener was walking Betty home from a local dance, and Jack, bitter that his girl-friend had been taken from him, followed a little way behind them. The gardener dropped Betty off at her father's house, left her, and was never seen again. There was a woman who later claimed to have found a head, and a man cutting a drainage ditch that claimed to have found a man's bones, but nothing came of either.

Jack Slipe married Betty, and was the servant of a man named Jooasep (Joseph) Tyson, who suspected he had killed the gardener, but he never confessed. He died before he was an old man. The implication seems to be that the Oxenfell Dobby is a remnant of the gardener being murdered on his way home from dropping Betty off.

A lot of the stories collected by Gibson seem to bear a lot of the hallmarks of Victorian ghost stories, without those unique to northern English folklore (apart from words like *dobby*). His writings therefore do not provide a full picture of the beliefs of ordinary people, and in any case were published quite late-on. Having said this, it is certainly possible (even likely) that the popular ghost stories of the Victorian period did have some

[41] It seems as though Gibson may have had a preference for stories about women called Betty.

effect on the ghost stories that people told one another in these corners of northern England, playing upon pre-existing local concepts to express themselves in a slightly different way.

Every system of folklore makes perfect sense in its cultural context, although it can seem alien from the outside. Reading about any historical or extant structure of local beliefs is likely to elicit some emotional response in us, but we must be aware that these emotional responses are culturally conditioned.

Many of these concepts are still meaningful to people living in rural Cumbria. Although modern ideas will have shaped their interpretation of them, they still have direct or near-direct emotional connections to people who lived in the cultural landscape of these stories, and that cultural landscape in many ways still exists. The fells can still be startlingly remote, as can the lowland paths and drystone walls that many of us have wandered around.

These stories may appeal to us specifically because they are easy to layer emotional residue onto; because the concept of elves and goblins reminds us of something our favourite author has written, or something we have read in a book about the occult, or a translation of a Norse myth we have read. Most of the people who told these stories historically were aware of none of these things, and to make these connections is to *distance* ourselves from them. To gain the most representative understanding of them, we have to put ourselves, as far as possible, in the specific cultural environment that they were in. Although it would be nice to elaborate on this topic somewhere else in future, hopefully these brief and reductive chapters have gone a small way towards achieving that.

Þórr and Hymir fishing for Jörmungandr, from the Gosforth Cross.

My Experiences with the Dialect.

While I was raised in the south of England, my dad's side of the family is Cumbrian, and as a result I have had some exposure to the dialect, mostly as spoken by people older than me. My family is from the north-eastern part of Cumbria, in the area surrounding Penrith: my father and his siblings were born at Skelton, my grandparents were born in that general vicinity in the mid and late 1930s. It is probably my older relatives who have most influenced my interest in this subject.

I would describe my grandfather's pronunciation as on the tail end of later Cumbrian, with relatively little southern influence in terms of the actual vowel qualities. However, the arrangement of lexical sets depends on who he is talking to. Many older Cumbrians I know, including my grandfather, do something called **code-switching**, which all of us do on some level. Code-switching is where we automatically switch between different ways of speaking depending on our audience: we might automatically speak more formally to a teacher or employer, for example, or swear more around our friends. This applies to speech and behaviour.

Code-switching is more noticeable in people who speak more than one language natively; they will be able to switch between their languages without any effort, and without having to pay attention to each word to make sure they don't accidentally mix languages. The two languages are, if you like, in 'different places' in their mind; when they're in English mode, they will not accidentally use words from their second language, and vice versa. They will slip up occasionally, just as children will occasionally swear around their parents by accident, but it's automatic for the most part.

This also applies to speakers of more than one dialect. It's particularly noticeable in Germany and Scotland, where rural people (even younger people) may speak a dialect so far from standard that people in cities find it difficult to understand them. They will be able to automatically modify their speech as necessary. This seems to be what some older speakers do in terms of their lexical sets. To give an example from my grandfather: for words like *what* and *water*, he may code-switch between saying the more standard /wɒt/ and /'wɔːtə(r)/ around my sister and I, but will use /wɛt/ and /'wɛtər/ around other Cumbrians. He will use /hɐʊs/ and /nɐɪt/ around my sister and I, but more often /hʊus/ and /neɪt/ around other Cumbrians. He seems to do this totally unconsciously.

On the latter point: when I was younger and knew less about phonology and vowel articulation, whenever I heard older, broader-speaking Cumbrians say *house*, I interpreted it as being monophthongal /huːs/, even though its actual realisation was probably more like [hɐʊs] or [hʊus]. I did not know what 'monophthongal' meant, of course, but I interpreted the Cumbrian pronunciation of *house* as rhyming with my southern pronunciation of *goose*, even though the two did not rhyme in reality. My *goose* vowel is something like [ʉw], whereas the Cumbrian *house* vowel that I heard was more like [əʊ]. I was hearing it as a monophthongal sound, even though it was not one. Literary evidence, and probably the experience of a lot of Cumbrians nowadays, speaks to the same kind of experience: the Cumbrian *house* vowel is heard as a monophthong, even though in most accents it is a diphthong, and sometimes quite a wide one. It was, of course, monophthongal [uː] fairly recently, but it is not anymore. The same thing applies to the Cumbrian *neet* ('night') vowel, which used to be [iː] but is now [ei] or [əɪ].

I think we interpret these vowels as monophthongs because we compare them to the standard. The standard *house* and *night* vowels in British English are [aʊ] and [ʌɪ], which are very wide indeed; in comparison, the broad Cumbrian diphthongs are quite narrow, sometimes very narrow[42].

The breaking of /iː/ and /uː/ are interesting in another way as

---

[42] For a similar but separate example, see the Canadian stereotype of pronouncing 'about' as 'aboot': no speaker I know has this vowel as monophthong, but many outsiders perceive it as a monophthong. In this case, however, Canadian speakers generally do not perceive it as a monophthong.

well. They have broken according to a very similar, if not identical, pattern to how they did in the south during the great vowel shift. The vowel shift can be hard to imagine actually happening because of its scale and speed, and it can certainly be difficult to imagine that people at the time did not notice it. The breaking of the high vowels in Cumbrian over the last 120 years serves to show just how rapidly this sort of thing can happen without the average native speaker noticing any change.

The disappearance of unique Cumbrian vocabulary and the levelling of lexical set differences seems to have come as a result of this code-switching; native speakers have less and less reason to speak broadly, and so their ability to speak broadly diminishes from generation to generation. Younger speakers today sometimes retain older Cumbrian features of pronunciation, such as the absence of glottal reinforcement.

To tell whether you have glottal reinforcement, try saying the word *trap* slowly. A speaker with GR will hear that the *a* sound comes to an abrupt stop, and then there is a very brief moment of silence (without any air flow through the vocal tract) before the *p* is released. This is a feature of standard British English. On the other hand, for a speaker without GR, the *a* sound will not stop abruptly: there will be continuous airflow through the vocal tract until the /p/ is articulated. It's very, very hard to describe the difference without using audio examples; you may be able to find some online.

Younger Cumbrian speakers also vary in whether they pronounce certain vowels as monophthongs or diphthongs, for example in *stone* and *lake*. The older /jɐ/ sequence is gone in the *stone* set for most people under 30, but they may adhere to the wider northern tradition of pronouncing *stone* something like /stɔːn/, or they may take southern influence and pronounce it as a diphthong more like /stɜʊn/. Likewise, *lake* may be /leːk/ or /leɪk/. Speakers generally will either have both as monophthongs or both as diphthongs. Speakers with both as diphthongs are, in my limited experience, more likely to use a more velarised version of the /l/ phoneme ([ɫ]) in all positions, and to lack glottal reinforcement. There is marked regional variation in how well broader Cumbrian characteristics have survived.

In older and broader speakers, patterns of speech are much like they are in the Orton survey, and resemble the style in which a lot of the dialogue of 19th-century dialect literature is written. My grandfather, who I mentioned earlier, still generally uses an alveolar tap /ɾ/ as his rhotic consonant, and is more likely to speak rhotically if with other Cumbrians. He speaks largely non-rhotically in rapid speech with my sister and I, but when speaking slowly or enunciating, he will more often realise /r/ after vowels.

Since I was a child, I noticed that he had a peculiar habit. When he was finished talking, or sometimes when he was not talking at all, or occasionally when he was responding to something, he would say *aye*, and then would seem to 'breathe the word back in' - that is, to say it voicelessly while inhaling, rather than exhaling. I actually noticed myself doing it for a short while as a child, and still do from time to time. I thought for a long time that this was just a habit of his, until I spoke to an American who had once met an elderly Cumbrian who did the same thing. I researched it a bit, and found that these are called **ingressive sounds**, and they are used in several languages around the world, although they are usually not phonemes[43]. Ingressive sounds are speech sounds produced while the speaker is breathing in (most sounds are produced while breathing out). They are usually reserved for short words such as *yes* and *no*. My granda only ever pronounces *aye* ('yes') ingressively, and only ever in isolation. As for its origin - pronouncing *yes* in this way occurs in a variety of Germanic languages, including lots of dialects of English (mainly Irish and Scottish ones, and American ones derived thence), in northern German dialects, and in dialects of all known Scandinavian languages. Given this distribution, it could be put down as a Scandinavian feature, but it could also be a niche West-Germanic feature that has survived in certain pockets in northern Britain.

---

[43] That is, they're not normally used in ordinary speech - they're only used for certain stray words said in isolation.

In my early days of studying the dialect, before I had much linguistic knowledge or intuition, I often wondered whether later Cumbrian could be called a separate language to English. I think any contemplation like that, which I'm sure many people have, comes from a desire to have a distinct and unusual cultural identity. We are told - or, at least, it becomes apparent to us - that in order to be really culturally distinct, you need to speak a different language. Distinctions between languages have often been held up by seperatist groups (for example in Cornwall, Catalonia and Friesland) as evidence that there is a great enough distinction between two cultures to warrant a separation in countries.

While I have no strong opinion on the matter, I wonder if we sometimes make the mistake of thinking of entire countries as the smallest meaningful units of cultural and linguistic diversity. You would be forgiven for questioning whether they were even meaningful units at all. Somebody from northern rural Cumbria undeniably has more in common with somebody from rural Dumfries than with somebody from London. Two people from either side of the German/Austrian border might well find more in common with each other than the German might find with somebody from Hanover. If you were to show somebody a linguistic map of Europe to an alien, and tell them to try to divide it up into countries, you might find they missed the mark completely. Cultural groups are dynamic things, and membership of a cultural group is extremely difficult to categorise. There will be people who consider everybody in the UK to be British and nothing more; there will be people who consider everybody in England to be English and nothing more; there will be people in Madrid who consider themselves to be culturally affiliated with both Madrid and Spain as a whole; there will be people who view themselves as European, as North American or as African, and people who view themselves as part of a far smaller cultural unit. Whether or not broad northern English and southern English were different languages in the 19th century, the cultural diversity within and between the speech communities was immense - far more immense, for example, than films and books set during the period tend to make out.

Although we are more connected and less isolated nowadays, and the cultural differences have been diluted somewhat, there is still something to be said for respecting the traditions that survive, and there is rarely any harm in taking an interest.

On a more experiential level, I sometimes wonder whether the things I associate with Cumbria are actually Cumbrian things, or whether they are specific to the environment I was in when I visited Cumbria as a child. There are aspects of the visceral experience of being in Cumbria that all locals will certainly know, and which will be shared by anybody who lives in a similarly upland-dominated part of the world: a certain coldness to the air, a certain bitterness to the water, an awareness that the weather can change very dramatically in not much time at all, which on some level can be said of anywhere in Britain. I have been in the fells and seen it go from bright, hot sun to stinging hail in something like thirty-five seconds, but again, this is an experience shared by anybody who lives in a similar part of the world. Some things will certainly be particular to my grandparents' house; the smells of tea tree oil, unglazed ceramic, paint and so on.

Bear in mind also that a lot of the experiences described in literature such as the *Memorandum* are unique to people living, for instance, before widespread mechanisation. Even into the 1940s, my grandfather recalls horses and traps being the primary way of getting around, although tractors were very much in use by then. The everyday smells and sounds of any part of Britain during the 18th century would obviously have been vastly different to the equivalent smells and sounds today. There would have been no traffic noise; horses would have been everywhere; clothes would have smelled of linen; everywhere even remotely near a dwelling would have smelled of chimney smoke. These would have been the things a modern person would notice if they were transported back in time, in any case: a person accustomed to them would have long since tuned them out. A native of the time may have more readily picked up smells that were seasonal;

particular vegetables or meats which were only available at certain times, or the metallic mown-grass smell of a sickle that has just been used to reap.

Again, though, these were European universals in the 18th century. Perhaps the smells of the moorland would have been more locale-specific, or the smell of burning peat. The tastes of particular meals, some of which are still eaten[44]. The experience of being among fells would have been uniquely northern (although open moorland exists in the south as well), but this is another thing to which locals are accustomed.

What spirituality I have comes from my grandmother, and it vaguely aligns with certain older aspects of folklore that I touched upon earlier in the book, but in many ways is far broader, having been inspired by her experience with a wide variety of people. It does not feel entirely right to go into detail about them here in this semi-academic and very public context. In any case, this spirituality is filtered through a modern lens, and should not be assumed to be identical to the cosmological ideas of a person living in the 19th century or earlier.

Much of the dialect literature was written before the Lake District became a popular tourist destination, and this must often bear on a modern person's experience: Windermere and Keswick are now designed for visitors. The fells are presented as a treasure of the English countryside, and the people who maintain them are often forgotten about or viewed as a nuisance. Without veering too far into politics, the process by which the rest of England 'claimed' the Lake District in the 19th century

---

[44] Tatie pot is particularly good. It is a stew made from potatoes, carrots, turnips, onions, black pudding, pork (preferably on the bone) and water. My grandmother would have cut each component into very large chunks, ensuring that the potatoes lay largely on the top and sprinkling them lightly with flour. I'm sure that people would argue that lamb is the proper meat to use (probably being the only meat readily available to certain people a couple of centuries ago).

strikes me as quite colonially-minded. Accommodation of visitors and incomers has certainly never been a problem, and the tourism industry has upheld the local economy in times when the sheep-farming economy has gone into decline. However, Cumbria has often been viewed as a resource to be used, with no mind paid to the people that have always lived there. Manchester City Council has twice decided it appropriate to flood already-inhabited Cumbrian valleys in order to provide water to the city. Ancient villages now exist as rubble at the bottom of Haweswater reservoir, occasionally re-emerging when the water level gets low enough during hot summers. Sustainable developments by local farmers are blocked in the name of national heritage. To paraphrase James Rebanks, enjoyment of the Lake District has been conflated with ownership of it. The same can surely be said of many other beautiful places in the world.

Leaving that aside, the experiences recounted to me by members of my family have been numerous, as well. Without prompting, a relative of mine once told me that when he was about ten, an elderly woman had held out both her hands cupped together and told him that it was a 'gowpen' - a word recorded in the *Glossarium Brigantinum*. He has told me that rabbits used to be snared and sold, and that if there was not much food to hand, a rook or two might be brought in from the garden to eat. He has spoken about the string of meals that used to be eaten during the working day, particularly at hay-time. As a matter of fact, I think the picture on the front cover of this book is of his grandparents during hay-time. He's spoken about the war, and how he hardly noticed it was happening (presumably because of a combination of him being a child and nobody having any reason to bomb rural Cumbria). He's spoken about his father digging graves for the church at Sowerby Hall, and about how he would have been glad to have soil as loose and workable as that at Penrith - the soil at Sowerby Hall, he said, was full of hard clay and stones. My granny, while she was alive, told me stories of the pig that her immediate family shared with her uncle during the war - they all chipped in to feed it, and when it was slaughtered, they took half each. My father has told me about the building of a house adjacent to the rectory in Skelton, which is still there now, and about the wood that had been there beforehand. Some timber men had paid them to allow them to come and cut the trees down, but the trees had all been rotten and full of rooks.

But these are stories for elsewhere, and I do not want to recount them in too much detail without consulting those who told them to me. I very much appreciate you reading this book, and I will leave you with a few bits and pieces to finish off with.

Turns of Phrase.

The following are some Cumbrian expressions, most of them from Prevost and Dickson-Brown, but some from older members of my family.

Auld keall ur seuner warm't ner new'uns meade.
'Old kale is sooner warmed up than new kale is made.' An old relationship or courtship more easily re-appears than a new one spontaneously appears.

Feckless fwok are aye fain.
'Stupid people are always happy.'

Seldom cu' t'better.
'Seldom comes the better.' Implies that change is rarely an improvement to the current situation.

Let that yar sit.
Yar meaning 'hare' - said when somebody is criticising somebody else or telling an unkind story about them. The 'hare' is the victim.

Better a la'al buss nor nea bield.
'Better a small bush than no shelter.'

Sheep are either dead, or trying to die.
I heard this one from my granda. Implies that sheep are not very good at keeping themselves alive.

It's a dree rwoad 'at hes nivver a turn.
'It's a dry road that never has a turn.'

Whooar t'lamb sucks, there it will be.
'Where the lamb sucks, there it will be.' Refers to Herdwick lambs, who remain *heftit* to the place they were raised.

Ken yersel and your neighbours'll nut misken ye.
'Know yourself and your neighbours won't mis-know you.' If one is sure of oneself, everybody else will be, as well.

Et hev a beann in yan's leg.
'To have a bone in one's leg.' Lazy people are often humorously said to fall over at the first sign of work, complaining of a 'bone in their leg.'

Et smell iv t'tnife.
'To smell of the knife.' Implies food is cut very thinly, and smells more of the knife it was cut with than of the actual food.

There are live stock and dead stock.
Another one from my grandfather.

His nwose wad split a hailstyan.
'His nose would split a hailstone.' Said of a person with sharp or defined features.

Fit et skin a paddock.
'Fit to skin a toad.' Said of a strong wind.

He'd be war if he ailed owt.
Said of somebody suspected to be feigning sickness - 'He'd be in a worse condition if he was actually ill.'

Selected Text I: Bede's Death Song.

There is no fragment of the Northumbrian dialect of Old English accessible to us that is identifiable as 'Old Cumbrian,' but it is unavoidably true that later Cumbrian is descended from Northumbrian Old English. The first text is the supposed final words of the Anglo-Saxon historian Bede, a Northumbrian man who died in 735 in what is now Tyne-and-Wear. A version of this text exists in the West Saxon dialect (the dialect most often used in textbooks), so we can compare forms, although bear in mind that a lot of the differences will come down to spelling. I will first provide the original text (St. Gallen manuscript 254) in Northumbrian, and then a word-for-word translation, and then an idiomatic translation to modern English.

Fore them neidfaerae   *naenig uuiurthit*
thoncsnotturra   *than him tharf sie*
to ymbhycggannae   *aer his hiniongae*
huaet his gastae   *godaes aeththa yflaes*
aefter deothdaege   *doemid uueorthae.*

Before the needjourney   none becomes
aware   [more] than him [that] must
to consider   before his going-hence
what for his spirit   good or evil
after [his] death-day   deemed will-be.

'Before the inevitable journey, nobody is wiser than he who is compelled to consider, before he sets off, which of his actions will be deemed good and evil after he has died.'

Several likely differences in pronunciation can be gleaned between the Northumbrian version and the West Saxon version, which I have not reproduced here for the sake of brevity. As is common in Northumbrian texts, word-final unstressed -*e* is often rendered as -*ae*, which probably represents a more open vowel. West Saxon *gaste* is reflected by Northumbrian *gastae*; WS *weorþe* is reflected by Nth. *weorthae*. In IPA, this difference was probably something along the vague lines of [ˈweorðe] vs. [ˈweorðæ] or [ˈweoʁðæ] - in modern terms, comparable to the difference between an RP and a Scouse pronunciation of *butter*. The word *death,* rendered in WS as *deaþe*, is *deoth-* in Nth. This is probably a reflection of a feature noted by Fulk in his *Introductory Grammar of Old English* (p121-2); certain Northumbrian varieties seem to have retained rounding on the second element of the diphthong that in WS was /æɑ/. The proto-Germanic form of this diphthong was probably /ɑu/, so something like /æu/ or /ɛu/ is probably a better representation of the Northumbrian diphthong in this instance.

The spelling of the vowel in the word *deemed* is also worth making an example of. The WS spelling is *demed*, the Nth. spelling *doemid*. This reflects a well-attested preservation of the front quality of the i-mutated vowel /eː/ in certain contexts in northern Old English, so that the word would have been pronounced something like /ˈdøːmid/ or /ˈdøːməd/. This rounding has left no mark on later Cumbrian.

The present tense third-person verb ending of WS *weorþan* - which in the WS translation is given as -*eþ* - is -*it* in the original Nth., hence *uuiurthit*, comparable to Middle High German *wirdet*.

Selected Text II: The Reeve's Tale.

Much earlier in the book, I discuss the Ellesmere manuscript of Chaucer's *Reece's Tale*, one of the *Canterbury Tales*. The manuscript was written in the early 1400s, and contains a southerner's depiction of a dialogue between northern men, which I will reproduce here:

'Aleyn! welcome,' quod Symkyn, 'by my lyf,
And Iohn also, how now, what do ye heer?'
'Symond,' quod Iohn, 'by god, nede has na peer;
Hym boes serve hym-selne that has na swayn,
Or elles he is a fool, as clerkes sayn.
Oure manciple, I hope he wil be deed,
Swa werkes ay the wanges in his heed.
And forthy is I come, and eek Alayn,
To grynde oure corn and carie it ham agayn;
I pray yow spede us heythen that ye may.'
'It shal be doon,' quod Symkyn, 'by my fay;
What wol ye doon whyl that it is in hande?'
'By god, right by the hopur wil I stande,'
Quod Iohn, 'and se how that the corn gas in;
Yet saugh I never, by my fader kyn,
How that the hopur wagges til and fra.'
Aleyn answerde, 'Iohn, wiltow swa,
Thanne wil I be bynethe, by my croun,
And se how that the mele falles doun
In-to the trough; that sal be my disport.
For Iohn, in faith, I may been of your sort;
I is as ille a miller as are ye.'

***

In the translation, pay attention to differences in vocabulary, as
well as places where the wording of the original text might have
seemed to mean something different to the actual translation.

'Aleyn! welcome,' said Simkin, 'by my life,
And John also, how now, what are you doing here?'
'Symond,' said John, 'by god, need has no rules;
He must serve himself that has no servant,
Or else he is a fool, as clerks say.
I expect our manciple will be dead,
The teeth in his head hurt so much.
And so I have come, and also Aleyn,
To grind our corn and carry it home again.
I pray you speed us through as fast as you can.
'It shall be done,' said Symkym, 'by my faith.
What will you do while it's in hand?'
'By god, I will stand right by the hopper,'
Said John, 'And watch how the corn goes in;
By my father's kin, I've still never seen
How the hopper wags to and fro.'
Aleyn answered, 'John, if you're going to do that,
Than I'll be beneath, by me head,
And see how the flour falls down
Into the trough; that shall be my sport.
For John, in faith, I may been of your sort;
I am as bad a miller as you are.'

The excerpt tells of two men that go to visit a miller to have their corn milled. They claim they wish to watch the corn go in and the flour come out, but this may be to prevent the miller, Symond, from stealing some of the flour as it comes out (or some of the grain as it goes in). The exact regional variety this text is supposed to represent is not clear - the place of origin of the characters is only given as 'somewhere in the north.'

Many characteristically northern forms occur here, deliberately placed by Chaucer. He uses *ay* for *always* (the same *ay* that has come to mean 'yes' in modern northern dialects). He uses *forthy* for *therefore*; this very word is given in the *Glossarium Brigantinum* as being characteristically Cumbrian (or possibly more broadly northern).

This particular manuscript spells *home* as *ham*, but the Hengwrt manuscript (possibly produced by the same author) has it as *heem* in the same place. As discussed earlier in this volume, this suggests a pronunciation something like /hɛːm/ - exactly what we would expect as a common ancestral form of later northern English and Scottish variants. *Father* is spelled *fader*, indicating a lack of intervocalic fronting, a feature of the later Cumbrian word *fadder*. It appears in the phrase *my fader kyn*, which notably lacks the genitive ending -*s*, also a feature of later Cumbrian. The prepositions *til* and *fra* are used for *to* and *from*. *Sal* is given rather than *shall* or *schal*, indicating an alveolar realisation of what would normally be /ʃ/ in standard English and Middle English. Such realisations seem to have been common in northern Middle English, even as far south as Norfolk, and certain occurred in later Cumbrian.

The line *swa werkes ay the wanges in his heed* shows the levelling of verb conjugation that I describe in the section on syntax and usage; the usual form of *werkes* would be *werken*. The same can be said of the final line of the except; *I is as ille a miller*, rather than *I am as ille a miller* or *I be as ille a miller*.

Selected Text III: Watermill Indenture.

This is an excerpt from a 1434 indenture, made at Carlisle, regarding the building of a watermill. I have found it in the Middle English Grammar Corpus, compiled by researchers at the University of Stavanger.

This indentur, made at karlell in þe festes of Philip day & Jacob þe yher of our lorde kynge henr sext of his renyng þe xij bythwen william of Denton Mair of þe Citi of karlell on þe ane parte & Johonn lyghtefut Carpentari on þe vthir part bers witnes þt it is acordid bithwene forsaid william & Johon þt the forsaide Johon sal mak a watiremylnn at Caldewbrigende sufficienli in al wryghte note þt fals to his craft. þ t is to say, in hewynge, in sawynge & in fellynge And ye forsaid william sal fynd al þe cariages & woodelefe; And þe forsaid william sal pay to þe forsaide Johon for his wrightenot & his trawell for þe said Miln Cvj s viij d . þt is to say xl s at byginnynge of his wark; & xxxiij s iiij d at mydes of his wark & xxxiij s & iiij d at ende of his wark; The whilk watiremyln sal be made complet & sufficientli ganging by þe fest of saynt Martin in wyntir next folowynge eftir þe dat of þis present indentur.

'This indenture, made at the city of Carlisle in the feasts of Philip and Jacob, in the twelfth year of the reign of Henry VI, between William of Denton, mayor of the city of Carlisle, one the one part and John Lightfoot carpentry on the other part, bears witness that it is agreed between the forsaid William and John that the forsaid John shall make a watermill at Caldewbrigend in every aspect that his craft covers - that is to say, in hewing, in sawing and in felling - and the forsaid William shall find [and presumably hire] all the carriages [involved in the construction of the mill] and wood; and the forsaid William shall pay to the forsaid John for his work and his travel for the said mill 106 shillings and 8 pence, that is to say 40 shillings at the beginning of his work, 33 shillings and 4 pence in the middle of his work and 33 shillings and 4 pence at the end of his work. The said watermill shall be made complete and sufficiently working by the feast of saint Martin in the winter that follows after the date of this present indenture.'

This text shows numerous features characteristic of later Cumbrian, including some that are also seen in text II. The name *Carlisle* is given as *karlell*, suggesting an indistinct vowel (probably /ə/) in the second syllable. This represents the first step in the reduction of the word to its later Cumbrian form, /ˈkɐɾəl/ or /ˈkerəl/.

The words *shall* and *make* and spelled *sal* and *mak*; the former is found variously in northern Middle English texts and is discussed in the notes following text II. *Mak*, with a short vowel, is found throughout later Cumbrian texts and in the speech of broader speakers today. It is sometimes *mek*, particularly in speakers from north-eastern Cumbria.

I cannot work out exactly where *Caldewbrigende* is, but it is presumably on the river Caldew, which flows from Skiddaw through Carlisle, and actually passes through a number of villages that members of my family have lived in at one time or another, namely Caldbeck /ˈkɔːdbek/, Hesket Newmarket /ˈheskət njuːˈmɐrkət/ and Sebergham /ˈsebrəm/.

The spellings of *al* ('all') and *fal* ('fall') are indicative that the final consonant in both words has not yet disappeared, as it does shortly after the great vowel shift in many Cumbrian varieties. *Work* is given as *wark*, indicating a pronunciation consistent with later Cumbrian /wɐrk/. The word *whilk* is used, which persisted into the 19th century, and meant *which*. Rather than *going*, the author uses the word *ganging*; the word *gang* continued to be used to that end in later Cumbrian. Finally, the word *after* is spelled with an initial *e-*, suggesting a pronunciation something like the later Cumbrian /ˈeftər/.

Selected Text IV: Agnes Wheeler's Dialogues.

This is an excerpt from a 1790 book by an Agnes Wheeler, in which she presents three dialogues in the Cumbrian. Specifically, this is from the second dialogue, in which three women discuss the loss of a husband.

Betty: *Whya haw er yee oa hear, I wod hae cum et seea afore naw, but it hes been sae caad, I was terrable feard a meaakin me sel badly agayn, en Ive hed a fearful Time ont for sure.*

Aggy: *Yee hev indeed, en yee leak fearful badly; cum en sit yee dawn ith Neak, en keep yer sel warm.*

Jennet: *Let me sweep upth Fireside, this rotten Tow meaaks us aw Dirt; dunnet sit thear Betty, for when th Dure hoppens awth Seat (soot) and th Reek el blaw ea yer Feace: Kem awt yer Haar Mudder, an put on yer Cap, what a seet yee er.*

Aggy: *Dear me Barn, I dunnet mitch heed me sel, I hae lost aw me Cumfort ea this Ward.*

Betty: *Aye, here hes been a girt awteration sen I wur here.*

Aggy: *Aye, waist omme! I hev hed a saar Loss, I hev parted wie a varra gud Husband, oh dear! Oh! Oh!*

Betty: *What yee munnet greet, but mack yer sel Content, its Gods will; we mun oa gang yaa Time er udder, I racken.*

Jennet: *I oft tell me Mudder shees rang to freat, mony a yans wars of than us, shees a varra gud Hause en two conny Fields, a Moss an a varra gud Garth, for Kaws, a Coaf, a Galoway, twenty Sheep, en a varra gud Swine, et dunnet want aboon a Week et been fat enuff ta kill; we hae baith Meal en Maut ith*

***

While reading the excerpt, try to pay attention to the author's use of orthography. The text is written in a version of Cumbrian with several archaic (even at the time) features.

Betty: Why, how are you all here? I would have come to see before now, but it's been so cold, I was afraid of making myself sick again, and I've had a frightening time of it, for sure.

Aggy: You have indeed, and you look very worse-for-wear; come and sit down in the corner, and keep yourself warm.

Jennet: Let me sweep the fireside, this rotten two makes us all dirty; don't sit there, Betty, because when the door opens, all the soot and the smoke will blow in your face: comb your hair, mother, and put on your cap, what a sight you are.

Aggy: Dear me, child, I don't look after myself, I've lost all my comfort in this world.

Betty: Yes, there has been a great alteration since I was [last] here.

Aggy: Yes, woe is me! I've had a painful loss, I've parted with a very good husband, oh dear! Oh! Oh!

Betty: You mustn't cry, but make yourself content, it's God's will; we must all go at one time or another, I reckon.

Jennet: I often tell my mother she's wrong to fret; many people are worse off than us, she's got a very good house and two lovely fields, a bog and a very good yard, four cows, a calf, a galloway [pony], twenty sheep, and a very good pig, that will be fat enough to kill in a week; we have both flour and malt in the

Ark, en part of a Flick a Bacon, beside a Net ful a Fleaks, en plenty a Potates: Soa then yee kna thur can be nae Want.

Betty: *Ise fain et hear it, en thau mun stay et Heaam, en be a good Lass, en cumfort the Mudder, en keep the sel unwed en tae can.*

Jennet: *Ise dea me best.*

Betty: *What il yee keep awth Swine, er yeel sell sum ont, yee can nivver dea wie it oa.*

Aggy: *Nay Ise sell o'th Legs an a Flick, en keepth rest; Ive a deal to think on naw sen I lost my poor Man, he oaways used tae butch it his sel, but naw I mun pay for it been dun: Nae weast me! What a girt Loss I hev on him, he was sean gean ith End, thof he hed meand him this hoaf Yeer en hed a girt Caadness in his Heaad, en wod oft tak awt his Pocket-neck-clath an lig it on his Heaad, en he thout it meaad it yeasy, I sewd him Flanin in his Neet Cap, but oa wod nit dea, I wod fain hev hed him hae hed a Docter, but nin oa his side, neither Men Fowk nor Wimmen, ivver hed yan, en he wod bring up nae new Customs, en I racken they cud hev dun him nae gud.*

Betty: *Nae net they, they er fit for nin but girt Fowk, et hes Brass enuff tae gie em; when my lile Barn was bornt, et it varra Guts was seen, we sent for yan, en what she deed, en monny a yan sed, en I hed ligd on enuff a Porposs Oil, she wod hae ment. What ye er for mackin Saals er net yee? Ea sum eth Ky en Sheep.*

Aggy: *Aye I hev maar en I can dea with, I'll keep nowt but yaa Kaw andth Galoway, it will be far less Trubble, I cannit dea wieth Land; a Woman is whaint ill of when shees left alaan, but me Cusen Giles promises ta dea for mea.*

ark, and part of a flitch of bacon, beside a netful of flounders, and plenty of potatoes: with that in mind, there can be no want.

Betty: I'm glad to hear it, and you must stay at home, and be a good girl, and comfort your mother, and keep yourself unmarried as best you can.

Jennet: I'll do my best.

Betty: What, will you keep all the pigs, or sell some of them? You can't deal with everything you have.

Aggy: No, I'll sell all the legs and a flitch, and keep the rest; I've a lot to think about now since I lost my poor husband. He always used to butcher it himself, but now I have to pay for it to be done: woe is me! What a great loss I've had, he went very quickly in the end, though he had complained for the last year of a great coldness in his head, and would often take his neck-cloth out of his pocket and lie it on his head, and he thought it eased it a bit, I sewed him [???] in his night cap, but it wasn't enough, I would gladly have let him have a Doctor, but nobody on his side [of the family], neither men nor women, had ever had one, and he didn't want to bring in any new customs, and I reckon they couldn't have done him any good.

Betty: No, they couldn't, they're good for none but posh people that have enough money to give them; when my little child was born, as soon as any sign of it was seen, we sent for one, and what she did, and many of them said, and I had put on enough porpoise oil, she would have told me to. What, you'll be making some sales, won't you? Of some of the cows and sheep.

Aggy: Yes, I have more than I can do [anything] with, I'll keep nothing but one cow and the galloway, it will be far less trouble, I can't do with land; a woman is very badly-off when she's left alone, but my cousin Giles promises to help me.

***

This text is extraordinarily useful, in that it gives us an extreme example of a conservative form of Cumbrian that lies away from the main course of development: a 'dead end' form of the dialect that was eventually overtaken by the version(s) that I have described elsewhere in this book.

The clearest archaic feature is the vowel in words like *maar* ('more') and *saar* ('sore'), which are spelled as though they retain a very similar pronunciation to their Old English forms *mār* and *sār*. Elsewhere in Wheeler's dialogues, this extends to words like *maad* ('made'), *paaper* ('paper'), *saak* ('sake'), *waak* ('awake'), and *faaver* ('favour'), indicating a quality similar to the Middle English one in the south, and certainly the Middle English one in parts of the north as well, judging by the typical spelling of words like *made* (often identical to the modern spelling, even in the north). Even in words like *goupen*, the diphthong has sometimes apparently been smoothed, giving *gaapen* ('two hands').

Wheeler spells with the digraph <ea> a sound that I confidently interpret as /iː/; both because she uses it in positions where /iː/ makes sense developmentally and because that digraph was used to spell /iː/ in most varieties of southern English at that time. She uses it to spell the preposition *i* ('in'), suggesting that people pronounced that word with its full vowel quality wherever it was used, or at least enough that the writer was *aware* of its full vowel quality. She uses it - often unsupplemented by other letters - to spell words in the *book* lexical set, suggesting a pre-diphthongisation quality in that set so that *book* is pronounced /biːk/, as it is in some Scottish dialects. It's not inconceivable that the sound might actually have been a marginal diphthong like /iɐ/, and that the author might just have seen no alternative way of spelling this sound. Words in the *stone* set are spelled sometimes with the trigraph <eea> and sometimes with the digraph <ea>. The former of these might be interpreted as /iɐ/, or something like it. The occurrence of the latter might suggest a partial merger of the *stone* and *book* lexical sets, or it might just be a matter of orthographic inconsistency; the book begins, after all, with a reminder that rendering dialect speech in writing is very difficult for orthographic reasons, as well as an apology for any mistakes the writer might have made as a result of her being a woman (even though she does a much better job of being orthographically consistent than many 19th-century writers).

The vowel in the word *house* is spelled with the digraph <au>; that in *now* is spelled with <aw>. This suggests a more southern pronunciation like /ɛʊ/, rather than the more common Cumbrian /uː/.

The word *night* is given as *neet*, with no indication of a palatal fricative. The disappearance of the fricative had probably happened in a lot of (if not most) northern varieties by this time as a result of southern influence, but Dickinson's description of 'an aspiration' probably present in the early 19th century tells us that it had not reached all dialects at the time Wheeler was writing. Notwithstanding, Wheeler's dialect must have lost the palatal consonant *after* the great vowel shift (or at the very earliest, towards the end of it), or *neet* would not be in the *see* lexical set.

Along the same lines, *though* is spelled *thof*, indicating unambiguously the development of /x/ in that lexical set. I am not aware of *thof* in any other texts, but the change from /x/ to /f/ elsewhere is evidenced by words like *slafter* ('slaughter') and the more standard *enough* ('enough').

The definite article is given as *th* throughout, often attached to the end of the previous word (as *t* often is in later Cumbrian). Joseph Relph's poetry, written some 40 years earlier, has various stages of the definite article (*the*, *th* and *t*), so it's clear that the 18th century was a period of change in that regard.

The spelling of the word *awteration* ('alteration') makes it clear that at some stage, the /l/ in that lexical set has been velarised, allowing for it to be vocalised in Wheeler's speech (or the speech of at least one of her characters).

In terms of grammar, a couple of constructions are worth noting. The first is *he hed meand him* ('he had complained'). Here, the word *mean* is cognate with English *moan*, but the feature of interest is the *him* that comes afterwards. In this sentence, the word *mean* seems to be treated reflexively - that is, the person doing the complaining is the same as the person being 'complained.' A(n ungrammatical) way of forming this construction in standard English would be 'he'd complained himself for the last year' (as opposed to the more grammatical, non-reflexive 'he'd complained for the last year').

The reflexive use of *mean* is not the only non-standard thing here; the pronoun would normally be the compound form *hissel* ('himself') in later Cumbrian, but is simply given as *him* here. Simple forms of reflexive pronouns that do not end in *-self* are often found in Middle English texts (see the paper by Ogura in the 'further reading' section for more), but rarely in modern ones. Finally, some interest lies in this sentence:

> ...*a varra gud Swine, et dunnet want aboon a Week et been fat enuff ta kill.*
>
> (Lit.) ...a very good swine, that doesn't want above a week to be fat enough to kill.
>
> (Idio.) ...a very good swine, that will be fat enough to kill in no more than a week.

A lot of features of this are nonstandard; the use of *want* for *need* is still common today, and the very roundabout phrasing of statements like this is explained in the section on earlier writers' observations. What I'm interested in is that the infinitive of *be* is given as *been*; the equivalent of a modern English speaker saying something like, "To been or not to been."

Nominatives in Middle English were very commonly suffixed with *-en*, and so this form would not be surprising if the text had been written perhaps four hundred years earlier. That Wheeler does not regularly mark infinitives in this way tells us that it's not a productive feature of her dialect; it is probably just a fossil. The same sort of thing could be said of the still-used word *gan* ('to go') which preserves an *-n* that used to be the infinitive suffix of the Old English word *gān*.

In terms of the historical value of the text, it reads like a genuine conversation that an ordinary woman has had with her friends. Whether Wheeler was actively transcribing a conversation or (perhaps more likely) recalling or inventing one that sounded natural to her, it gives us a rare glimpse into ordinary life. Where plenty of Cumbrian literature (and perhaps interactions with some older Cumbrians today) give an impression of relative indifference to loved ones dying, Wheeler gives an impression of a woman in a dire emotional state. The loss of her husband is clearly inseparably linked to the sudden overwhelming amount of re-arranging she must do, and they are spoken about interchangeably.

She gives a brief account of the possessions of somebody who is perhaps relatively poor, but not excessively so: a galloway pony, four cows etc. She also gives us some insight into the opinions an ordinary person might have had about doctors at that time. Aggy says that she 'gladly would have let him have a doctor,' which is in agreement with the sentiment in *Bobby Banks' Bodderment* that the woman of the household was in charge of finances by default.

The last paragraph of this excerpt implies that her husband took care of a large part of the farm work, whether directly or by subsidising it to employees, but that she is comfortably capable of looking after a small number of animals herself.

Selected Text V: Robert Anderson's Poetry.

This is a poem from the early 19th century by Robert Anderson, one of the more well-known dialect poets. It is entitled *The Cummerlan Farmer*.

I've thowt an I've thowt, ay, agean an agean,
Sin I was peet-heet, now I see it's qeyte plain,
We farmers er happier by far, tho' we're peer,
Than thur they caw gentlefwok, wid aw their gear;
Then, why about riches, aye meake sec a fuss?
Gie us meat, drink, an cleedin; it's plenty fer us -
Frae prince to the plewman, ilk hes but his day;
An when deeth gie's a beckon, we aw mun obey!

Our darrick's hawf-duin, ere the gentlefwok rise;
We see monie a lark dartin up to the skies;
An blithe as the burd sud aw honest fwok be -
Girt men gae their troubles, as offen as we!
Our weyves an our dowters, we wish to leeve weel;
They tnit, darn, an kurn, or they turn rock an reel;
Our sons niver grummel to toil by our seyde -
May happiness aye the industrious beteyde;

Our youngest lad, Dick, I yence tuik to the town,
He keek'd at shop-windows and sauntert aw roun,
"Aa, Fadder," says he, "sec a bussle an noise
May flay sair eneugh, aw us peer country bwoys!"
But seebem year aul, yet he daily wad work;
He'll sing owre to schuil, or he'll run to the kurk;
He lissens the parson, an brings heame the text,
I han him the beyble, but Dick's niver vext.

In storms, the peer beggars creep up to the fire,
To help sec as thur sud be ilk yen's desire;
They'll smuik a bit peype, an compleen ov hard teymes,

**

Try to pay attention to Anderson's portrayal of farmers and their attitudes to work; do you think he is romanticising their lifestyle, or presenting an honest account?

I've thought and I've thought, yes, again and again
Since I was very young, now I see it's quite plain:
We farmers are happier by far, though we're poor,
Than those they call 'gentle-folk,' with all their money.
Then why always make such a fuss about riches?
Give us meat, drink and clothing - that's plenty for us.
From a prince to a ploughman, each only has their lifetime;
And when death gives a beckon, we all must obey.

Our work is half-done before the rich people rise.
We see many a lark darting up to the skies:
All honest people should be as happy as birds -
Rich men have their troubles as often as we [do].
We wish to leave our wives and daughters well-off.
They knit and darn, and turn grindstone and reel.
Our sons never grumble to work by our sides;
May the industrious always be blessed with happiness.

Our youngest lad, Dick, I once took to the town.
He gazed at shop-windows and sauntered all round;
"Ah, father," he said, "Such a bustle and noise
"Might badly frighten us poor country boys!"
But seven years old, and he would work every day;
He'll sing the whole way to school, and run to the church;
He listens to the parson, and brings home the text;
I hand him the bible, but Dick's never vexed.

In storms, the poor beggars creep up to the fire;
To help the likes of them should be everyone's desire.
They'll smoke a bit [of] pipe, and complain of hard times,

Or tell teales of deevils that glory in creymes;
Expwos'd till aw weathers, they wheyles laugh an jwoke,
Breed, tateys, or wot-meal, we put in the pwoke;
Tho' some are impostors, and daily to bleame,
Frae princes to starvelins, we oft fin the seame.

Our 'squire wid his thousans, keeps jauntin about,
What, he'd give aw his gear, to get shot o' the gout -
Nowther heart-ache nor gout, e'er wi' rakin hed I,
For labour brings that aw his gowd cannot buy!
Then, he'll say to me, "Jacep, thou whissels an sings,
"Believe me, you've ten teymes mair plishure nor kings;
"I mean honest simplicity, freedom, an health;
Far dearer to man, than the trappings o' wealth!"

Can owt be mair sweet, than leyke larks in a mworn,
To rise wi' the sunsheyne, an luik at the cworn?
Tho' in winter, it's true, dull an lang er the neets,
Yet thro' leyfe, fwok mun aye tek the bitters wi' sweets.
When God grants us plenty, an hous'd are the crops,
How we feast on cruds, collops, an guid butter-sops -
Let yer feyne fwok in town brag o' denties whee will,
Content an the country fer mey money still!

They may bwoast o' their gardens as much as they leyke,
Don't flow'rs bloom as fair under onie thworn deyke?
The deil a guid beyte they wad e'er git, I trowe,
Wer't nit fer the peer man that follows the plough,
If we nobbet get plenty, to pay the laird's rent,
An keep the barns teydey, we aye sleep content;
Then ye girt little fwok, niver happy in town,
Blush, blush, when ye laugh at a peer country clown!

Or tell tales of devils that glory in crimes,
Exposed to all weathers, they laugh and they joke,
Bread, potatoes or oat-meal, we put in the poke.
Though some are imposters, and are daily to blame [for sth],
From princes to starvelings, we often find the same.

Our squire with his thousands keeps jaunting about,
But he'd give all his money to get rid of his gout -
Raking never gave me heart-ache or gout,
For labour brings things all his gold cannot buy!
Then he'll say to me, "Jacob, you whistle and sing,
"Believe me, you've ten times more pleasure than kings.
"I mean honest simplicity, freedom, and health;
"Far dearer to men than the trappings of wealth."

Can anything be more sweet than, like larks in the morning,
To rise with the sunshine and look at the corn?
Though in winter, it's true, dull and long are the nights,
Yet through life, people must always take the bitter with the sweet.
When God grants us plenty, and the crops are housed,
How we feast on cruds, collops, an good butter-sops -
Let your rich people in town brag of their nice things if they will,
Content and the country for my money still!

They may boast of their gardens as much as their like,
Don't flowers bloom as pretty under any thorn hedge?
I daresay they would never have a good bite [to eat],
Were it not for a poor man that follows the plough.
If we only get plenty, to pay the lord's rent,
And keep the children tidy as we sleep always content,
Then you rich little people, never happy in town,
Blush, blush, when you laugh at a poor country clown!

This is an interesting poem in terms of the way it presents its subject matter. It makes a hard distinction between poor farmers and rich townspeople, and the overarching point is clearly that the former are happier and better-off than the latter. It could easily be criticised for over-romanticising farm life, and for implying that people of low socioeconomic status should be grateful for that status. 19th-century art depicting working people is often criticised on a similar basis.

However, if the implication of such criticisms is that people were *not* satisfied with their socioeconomic position, this seems a peculiar idea to me. James Rebanks, a fell farmer well-known for his 2015 book *The Shepherd's Life*, describes, largely without romanticisation, his process of realising that people from more industrialised communities valued the idea of 'going somewhere' and 'doing something' with their lives - an idea that was shocking and alien to him, and that had never occurred to him as a child. Mirroring this, it is often difficult for people from modern, industrialised communities to wrap their (our) heads around the fact that people from traditional communities might *not* have any interest in leaving those communities. Faced with this attitude, we tend to look for explanations of it that match our own experience and understanding of the world, and we end up framing their preferences according to our own: we might say that they have been brainwashed by a system that wants to keep them in what we consider to be poverty; we might say that they are backwards and neophobic.

In reality, the now-prevalant (but by no means universal) desires to distance oneself from ones family, to gather experiences from around the world and to be markedly more successful (or successful in a markedly different way) than ones predecessors are relatively new. It's often seen as a point of importance to encourage people to do these things, and to praise or respect them when they do. We are obsessed with the ideas of 'better' and 'different.' You are not successful if you merely maintain the quality of life you were born with.

An 18th- or 19th-century rural Cumbrian would have had little reason to seriously want to live in a town; it would have meant being separate from the people they loved and the life they understood, and they may have felt as though they were severing a vital connection. That is not to say that they would have seen their own lives as the height of happiness and fortune; as recounted in the *Memorandum*, many families struggled to get through winter, and financial difficulties would have been widespread, especially in an industry so directly reliant on the climate. Things were certainly very difficult for many people. However, happiness is a far more complicated thing arising from more factors than just wealth and financial stability. It arises from social cohesion. In particular, it arises from the kinds of social cohesion that we are accustomed to.

Of course, these kinds of preferences would have been highly personal; it's certain that some rural Cumbrians would have longed in live in Carlisle or even Manchester and not to have to farm anymore, but I maintain that to dismiss this poem as entirely romanticism is probably not entirely fair.

Selected Text VI: Keaty Curbison Cat.

This poem was published in 1891 by Alexander Gibson, and marks itself as *an oald, oald stwory*. Its subject matter evokes the early 17th century, when alleged witches were still the subject of persecution in north-western England, but it is impossible to tell whether the story itself is that old.

Keaty Curbison' cat hed a whudderin' waow,
A waow like a yowl, fit to freeten a man,
An' t'leet iv it' e'e was a green glentin' lowe -
Iv it e'e, we may say, for it no'but hed yan.
T'ya lug hed been rovven, an' hung like a cloot,
While t'udder stack up like t'cockad iv a hat,
Lang whiskers like brussles spread o' roond it' snoot,
It wosn't a beauty - Keáte Curbison cat!

Keáty Curbison cat was a terror to t'toon -
Till butt'ry an' pantry it may'd hed a kay.
Intil ivery hoose, ayder up t'geát or doon,
By air-wole or chimla it wummelt it' way.
For thievin' an' reávin 'twas war' nor a fox,
Ther' wasn't a hen-hoose it hedn't been at;
Young chickens, an' geslins, an' pigeons, an' ducks,
Wer' "ghem, ga way tul't" to Keáte Curbison cat.

Keáty Curbison cat like a tiger wad feight;
When it' back was weel up an' o' ruddy for war,
It wad lick a cur dog mair nor ten times it' weight,
An' mongrels an' messans they dursn't cu nar.
It hed leet of a trap, an' ya feút was teán off,
An' it' tail hed been dock't - but it dudn't mind that,
It wad flee at owte whick 'at wad give it a lofe,
A hero, i' hair, was Keáte Curbison cat.

Pay attention to the use of prepositions, and to the absence (marked by the author with an apostrophe) of the possive -s ending found in standard English.

Katie Curbison's cat had a terrifying 'meow',
A 'meow' like a yowl, fit to frighten a man,
And the light of its eye was a green glinting flame -
Of its *eye*, we can say, for it only had one.
One ear had been ravaged, and hung like a clout,
While the other stuck up like the plume of a hat,
Long whiskers like bristles spread all round its snout,
It wasn't a beauty, Kate Curbison's cat!

Katie Curbison's cat was a terror to the town -
To buttery and pantry, it could have had a key.
Into every house, either up the road or down,
By air-hole or chimney it wriggled its way.
For thieving and raiding it was worse than a fox,
There wasn't a hen-house it hadn't been at;
Young chickens, and goslings, and pigeons, and ducks,
Were "game, go to it!" to Kate Curbison's cat.

Katie Curbison's cat like a tiger would fight;
When its back was arched up and all ready for war,
It would beat a cur dog more than ten times its weight,
And mongrels and lap-dogs dared not come near.
It had escaped from a trap, and one foot was taken off,
And its tail had been clipped, but it didn't mind that,
It would quickly run at anything that would give it a reason,
A hero, in hair, was Kate Curbison's cat.

Keáty Curbison cat hed of lives a lang lot -
Ye ma' toak aboot nine - it hed ninety an' mair;
It was preúf ageán puzzen or pooder an' shot -
They hed buriet it yance, but it still dudn't care.
It was tiet iv a meal-bad and flung into t'beck,
But t'bag it brong heám for it mistress a brat,
Limpin', trailin' 't ahint it wi' t'string round it' neck -
T'beck cudn't droon Keáty Curbison cat.

Keáty Curbison cat browte oald Keáty to grief -
Pooar body! she nowder was cumly nor rich -
An' t'neybors aboot settlet doon to t'belief
'At her cat was a divil an' she was a witch.
An' they said, "Let us swum her i' t'tarn," an' they dud;
She swom a lal bit, an' than droon't like a rat,
An' t'cat aboot t'spot swom as lang as it cud,
An' finish't at last was Keáte Curbison cat.

Katie Curbison's cat had of lives a long lot -
You may talk about nine, it had ninety and more;
It was strong against poison or powder and shot -
They had buried it once, but it still didn't care.
It was tied in a hessian sack and flung into the stream,
But the bag it brought home, an apron for its mistress,
Limping, trailing it behind it with the string round its neck -
The stream couldn't drown Katie Curbison's cat.

Katie Curbison's cat brought old Katie to grief -
Poor woman! She was neither well-off nor rich -
And the neighbours around here began to believe
That her cat was a devil and she was a witch.
And they said 'let's swim her in the lake,' and they did;
She swam a little bit and then drowned like a rat,
And the cat swam around that spot as long as it could,
And finished at last was Kate Curbison's cat.

***

The poem speaks largely for itself. A few finer features of the
phonology of the Cumbrian it is written in are evident: the
spelling of *wole* for 'hole' suggests that /hw/ sequences have been
reduced to /w/ for the author, which tells us that *whick* 'quick;
alive' would have been /wɪk/. The preposition *iv* is used several
times, mostly overlapping semantically with standard English
'of,' but on one occasion being used differently; the cat is said to
have been *tiet iv a meal-bag* ('tied [iv] a hessian sack'). This
reinforces the notion that *iv* can be used in some situations where
'in' and 'on' would be preferred in standard English. My
grandfather has told me a personal anecdote that bears spookily
close to this one in some ways, but this book is not the place to
divulge it.

Glossaries.

I will first provide an updated version of M. Walcott's 1870 abridgement of the 1677 *Glossarium Brigantinum*. I will provide the original spellings, alongside a broad IPA transcription of how the word is likely to have been pronounced in 1677 (bearing in mind the pronunciation may have changed by the later Cumbrian period), as well as a definition and an updated etymological examination for each word.

Glossarium Brigantium Abridgement

Aamery /'ɐːmə‿riː/ *n.* - A cupboard, a safe for meat. The initial part, *aam*, is the regular development from OE *ælm-*; 'alms, food given to the poor.' This later develops to *aumry* /ɔːmriː/.

Acram /'ɐkrəm/ *n.* - A situation possibly relating to the Anglo-Scottish wars which lasted into the late 1500s, in which a local clergyman was bound and left to watch a duel between a champion fighting on his behalf and an enemy. The author (either of the abridgement or the original *Glossarium*) is vague about what the outcome of this duel determined. The etymology is difficult to parse; it looks as though it is related to *acre*, which would make sense if the duels were related to land disputes, but this ought to be **yakker* in mainstream[45] Cumbrian at this point. It could be from a non-mainstream variety where the initial /j/ has been deleted, but I can make no confident assertions here.

Addle /'adəl/ *v.* - To earn through work. From ON *øðlask* 'to come into possession of property.'

Amell /ə'mel/ *prep.* - Between. From the ON prepositional phrase *á milli*, 'between.'

Anenst /ə'nenst/ *prep.* - Over, against. This can be *anent* in later

---

[45] By 'mainstream Cumbrian,' I mean that variety of Cumbrian that has formed the base for the phonological developments leading to the varieties of later Cumbrian.

dialect literature, and in Scots, with the meaning 'on top of.' Full etymology can be found in the chapter on syntax, but probably from unattested OE *onemned, 'on the same level as.'

Anters /ˈɛntərz/ *prep*. - If, perhaps. Hard to parse. Resembles Dutch *anders*, and the author suggests a connection, but it seems odd that a single Dutch loan word would make its way so far into the core vocabulary, and the /d > t/ sound change cannot be accounted for in this instance.

Arvel-bread /ˈɐːrvəl briːd/ *n*. - Bread or cake eaten at funerals. *Arvel* from ON *erfiǫl*, 'inheritance beer.'

Ask /ɐsk/ *n*. - A newt, according to the *Glossarium*, but later literature suggests *ask* meant 'lizard,' with a newt being a *watter-ask* ('water-lizard'). From OE *āðexe*, 'newt or lizard.' The word has clearly been subject to a lot of elision, perhaps being handed back-and-forth between dialects and at some point undergoing metathesis[46].

Astite /əsˈtəɪt/; /əsˈtɛɪt/; /əsˈteɪt/[47] *conj*. - As soon. Author suggests that the *-tite* element is from OE *tīd*, 'time.' The vowel development agrees with this; and the word-final /d > t/ change is common in Cumbrian, albeit not so much in this environment.

Attercop /ˈɛtər ˌkɒp/ *n*. - Spider. From OE *ātorcoppe*, 'spider.' The OE word ought to give Cumbrian *yattercop*; the vowel may have shortened before the great vowel shift, or this may be another example of a non-mainstream variety where initial /j/ is deleted. On the face of it the latter seems unlikely, as *attercop* appears in later dialect literature - but it is possible that later literature has just taken the word from the *Glossarium*.

Bane /bɛːn/ *adj*. - Ready. Clearly the same as *bain* in later dialect dictionaries, which (used of roads) means 'handy, convenient.' Its application may be even broader than this. From ON *beinn*,

---

[46] Metathesis is when two sounds switch places. The Cumbrian word *ex* ('ask') may have undergone a similar process of metathesis but in reverse, or it may simply be derived from an Old English form *acs* rather than *asc*; both are known from the literature.

[47] All three may be correct, depending on what stage in the diphthongisation process the vowel was.

'straight, direct.'

Barn /bɐːrn/ *n.* - A child. From OE *bearn*. The Scots form *bairn* /bɛːrn/ later entered the dialect as a loan word, but older Cumbrian literature always gives *barn*.

Beck /bek/ *n.* - A stream. The author specifies 'a mountain stream;' this may have been the meaning at the time, and it may have broadened to mean any stream later on. From ON *bekkr*, 'a brook or stream.'

Beeld /biːld/ *n.* - A shelter. Later literature gives the meaning of a stone house for sheltering in the fells. From OE *bēld*-, 'bold' and possibly later 'protective.'

Belten /ˈbeltən/ *n.* - May-day. Apparently from a Celtic language, and related to English *beltane*, of the same meaning.

Blake /blɛːk/ *adj.* - Bright blackish-brown (whatever that is supposed to mean). Later literature has it as a beige-like colour. From ON *bleikr*. Further etymology in the section on Scandinavian loan-words.

Blin /blɪn/ *v.* - To cease, stop. From OE *blinnan*, same meaning.

Bowr /bɐʊr/ *n.* - A parlour, living room. From OE *būr*, same meaning. This would normally have given **boor* /buːr/ by this stage, so it may be a borrowing from a more southerly dialect, where the great vowel shift had affected back vowels.

Brade of /brɛːd əv/ - To resemble. *Brade* from ON *bregda*.

Brigg /brɪg/ *n.* - Bridge. From OE **bryg*; unpalatalised form.

Brott /brɒt/ *n.* - Corn scattered at a barn door. From OE *gebrot*, 'fragment.' The OE *ge-* prefix is almost always lost in Cumbrian, as it is in standard English.

Bune-ploughs /buːn plʊxs/ *n.* - Ploughs of tenants. *Bune* probably from OE *gebunden*, 'bound;' the ploughs are 'bound' to the lend, rather than belonging to the tenants.

Byre /bəɪr, bɐɪr, beɪr/ *n.* - A cowhouse. From OE *býre*, 'hovel, shed.'

Clemmed /klemd, klemt/ *adj.* - Very thirsty. I list both forms because the past participle would certainly have had the /-t/ ending in some varieties by this time. Author suggests OE *beclæmed*. This is questionable; the OE root *clæm*- would give Cumbrian *clam*- (though this could be explained by dialectal difference or borrowing), and the word meant 'plastered or glued together' in OE. This meaning could conceivably have become 'thirsty,' in the sense that a thirsty person may feel that their mouth and throat are glued together, but this is a bit of a reach.

Cleugh or **clughe** /klɪəx/ *n.* - A ravine or breach down a hillside. Probably from unattested OE **clōh*, which agrees with the Scots and Dutch cognates. The alternative spelling offered by the author suggests an alternative, non-mainstream pronunciation.

Click /klɪk/ *v.* - To snatch, grab. Etymology unclear. Both an OE and an ON form could be conceived of, but both would be unattested.

Codd /kɒd/ *n.* - A 'pillar.' I am skeptical of this one. The author gives an Icelandic cognate, but the only comparable ON word is *koddi*, which means 'pillow.' I think it's conceivable that the author asked a Cumbrian speaker to translate the word and got the answer /ˈpɪlə/, the regular Cumbrian form of *pillow*, but which sounds like *pillar* if you're used to non-rhotic accents.

Cowp /kɛʊp/ *v.* - To exchange. From ON *kaupa,* 'to purchase.' Cognate of English *cheap*, via OE *cēap*.

Deeght /dɪçt/ *v.* - To winnow corn, to dress or clean. From OE *dihtan*, 'to arrange, prepare.'

Deft /deft/ *adj.* - Pretty. From OE *dæfte*, 'accommodating, gentle,' probably a dialectal form thereof, given the unexpected vowel. Correspondence between OE *æ* and Cumbrian /e/ is not unheard-of; compare *efter* ('after').

Dobby /ˈdɒbiː/ *n.* - A pathetic or weak old person, a folkloric being (see discussion in the section on folklore). Possibly from an unattested OE word such as **dobig*.

Doughty /ˈdɒxtiː/ *adj.* - Stout. From OE *dohtig*, 'strong, bold.'

Dree /driː/ *v.* - To bear something. From OE *adrēogan*.

Eeth /iːð/ *adj.* - Easy. Given as *eith* in Relph's *Miscellany*. From OE *ēaðe*, 'easy.'

Fain /fɛːn/ *adj.* - Glad, happy. From OE *fægen*, same meaning.

Fang /faŋ/ *v.* - To seize, take. From ON *fanga*, same meaning.

Fettle /ˈfetəl/ *n.* - One's state of being. To be in *giud fettle* is to be in good health or well-off. From OE *fetel*, same meaning.

Flite /flɑɪt, flɛɪt, fleɪt/ *v.* - To scold somebody. From OE *flītan*, 'to struggle, strive.'

Fluke /flɪək/ *n.* - A plaice fish. From OE *flōc*, 'flatfish.'

Flyre /flaɪr, flɐɪr, fleɪr/ *v.* - To laugh with scorn. The author suggests an Icelandic cognate *flýra* which would point to an ON origin, but I cannot find any such word with the same meaning.

Formal /fərˈmɐl/ *v.* - To be evidence of something. The *-mal* is from ON *mál* ('speech'), with the OE *for-* prefix attached. The sense could be to bespeak something, to metaphorically speak on behalf of it.

Forthy /fərˈðəɪ, -ðɐɪ, -ðeɪ/ *adv.* - Therefore. From OE *forþȳ (þe).*

Forwhy /fərˈʍəɪ, -ʍɐɪ, -ʍeɪ/ *adv.* - Wherefore; for which reason. From OE *forhwȳ (þe).*

Fremd /fremd/ *adj.* - Strange, unusual. From OE *fremd,* and cognate with German *fremd*, 'foreign, unusual.'

Gang /gɐŋ/ *v.* - To go. From OE *gangan.*

Geat /gɛət, giɐt/ *n.* - Path, way, road. From ON *gata*, 'road,' whose stressed vowel has been lengthened.

Geaveloc - Crowbar. The spelling implies a pronunciation like /ˈgɛəvəˌlək/ or /ˈgiɐvəˌlək/, which is in line with OE *gafeluc* ('pole; javelin'); this is another instance of a short vowel lengthening in an open syllable. The *-oc* suffix is diminutive, equivalent to the suffix at the end of words like *bollock, millock, bittock.*

Gif /gɪf/ *prep.* - If. From OE *gif.* This is a strange one, because although the word is reasonably well-attested in Cumbrian and on first glance seems to be an unpalatalised form, it is not reflected in other velar forms in other Germanic languages. It may be a freak case of Proto-Germanic /j/ velarising, perhaps via a dialectal loan, but that's probably clutching at straws a little bit. It may reflect an aspect of the palatalisation issue that I have not addressed or noticed.

Gill /gɪl/ *n.* - A narrow valley or ravine with a stream at the bottom. From ON *gil.*

Goupen /gɛʊpən/ *n.* - The amount held in both hands. Has several Scandinavian cognates, and is probably derived from ON one way or another[48].

Grave /grɛːv/ *v.* - To dig. This later exists in the parallel form *greav* /grjɐv/. Both are from OE *grafan*, the latter arising from a variant with a lengthened vowel.

Greet /griːt/ *v.* - To cry, weep. From OE *grētan*, same meaning.

Grupe /grɪəp/ *n.* - A sink. From OE *grōf,* 'trench, furrow.' Cognate with English 'groove.' The form given here has an errant 'p,' and may be a dialectal borrowing.

Hackin /ˈhɐkən/ *n.* - A pudding made from the innards of sheep or pigs. Equivalent to English *hack* + *ing*, from OE *haccian*, with the sense that the intestines have been hacked apart in order to make the pudding. This word is later used to refer a pudding of mincemeat and fruit.

Hag-worm /ˈhɐgwʊrm/ *n.* - A snake. Probably constructed by analogy to ON *hǫgg ormr* ('snake', lit 'striking worm'), but with the *worm* component being from OE *wyrm*, as the ON cognate lacks the initial /w/. In both OE and ON, the word 'worm' referred to worms, snakes and serpent-like mythical animals. It's an interesting case of people in another society taxonomising things in a different way than we would; snakes and worms looked and moved similarly, and so they were both categorised as worms. This would not have implied any genetic relationship; early medieval people did not think in those terms.

Haver /ˈhɐvər/ *n.* - Oats. From ON *hafri*. Entirely replaced the native *oats* as the standard word, with *oats* being reintroduced as a loan word in the Middle English or early Modern English period.

Heck /hek/ *n.* - The hatch or gate between a barn and a cowhouse. Used later to refer to a hatch or gate in general. From a dialectal variant of OE *hæca*, 'door-fastening, bolt.' This root also gives standard English *hake*.

Herry /ˈheriː/ *v.* - To rob. Related to 'harry,' as in 'the harrying

---

[48] It is at this point in the process that I began to realise that the author of the *Glossarium* sometimes helpfully provide Icelandic words that look vaguely similar to the Cumbrian word but have a completely different meaning.

of the north.' From OE *herian*.

Hie thee /həɪ ðiː, hɐɪ-, heɪ-, -ðə/ - A command to hurry up. The author gives OE *higan* as the ancestor of *hie*, which is developmentally sound, but no OE dictionary I can find lists *higan* as meaning anything plausibly connected to 'hurry.'

Hog /hɒg/ *n.* - A castrated male sheep between one and two years old. Possibly from ON *hǫggva*, 'to chop, hew.'

Gimmer /ˈgɪmər/ *n.* - A female sheep between one and two years old. From ON *gymbr*.

Hoven /ˈhɔːvən, ˈhwɔːvən/ *adj.* - (Of bread) leavened, raised. From a past participle of OE *hebban*. Was almost certainly taken as a loan word from another dialect during the Middle English period, as the Cumbrian reflex of OE *hōfen* ought to be /ˈhɪəvən/.

Hul /hʊl/ *n.* - A pigsty or calf house. Probably of the same derivation as standard English 'hull,' meaning the frame or body of a ship; the etymology is not entirely clear. There is an OE word *hulu*, attested as meaning 'husk.' My suspicion is that a second, unattested sense of the word may have existed; that of a body or external form. This could easily give the standard English and Cumbrian reflexes.

Keckle /ˈkekəl/ *v.* - To laugh. No clear OE root, but compare English *cackle*, German *gackern*, Dutch *kakelen*. Speaks to a possibly unattested OE ancestor.

Kenn /ken/ *v.* - To know. From OE *cennan*, 'to declare.' Cognate with Scots *ken* and German *kennen* ('to know (a person or thing)') among others.

Kep /kep/ *v.* - To catch. Author gives OE *ceppan*, but I cannot find this in any dictionary.

Ketty /ˈketiː/ *adj.* - Dirty. Possible from ON *kjöt*, 'meat, flesh, carrion,' but this in turn comes from PGmc **ketwą*, and I wonder whether it's possible that this gave an unattested OE form that better fits its reflex.

Kirk /kʊrk/ *n.* - A church. From OE unpalatalised *cirice* or ON *kirkja*; either works.

Kyte /kəɪt, kɐɪt, keɪt/ *n.* - The belly. Origin unclear; the author lists several possibilities, but none fit phonologically. Compare the word *brimmel-kyte* ('bramble berry').

228

Lake /lɛːk/ *v.* - To play. From ON *leika*, same meaning.

Lakons /ˈlɛːkənz/ *n.* - Playthings. Equivalent to *lake* + *ings*. Evidence that the gerund ending *-ing* (or *-and*, as the case may be) had been reduced to /-ən/ by 1677, because the author variously spells it *-in* and *-on* with no clear pattern.

Lathe /lɛːð, lɛəð/ *n.* - A barn. From ON *hlaða*, 'barn, storehouse.' Another subject of open-syllable lengthening.

Lave /lɛːv, lɛəv/ *n.* - The remainder, the rest. From OE *lāf*.

Lavrock /ˈlɛvrək/ *n.* - A lark. From OE *lāwerce*, probably mangled by interdialectal borrowings, because the /w/ - /v/ change is extremely unusual.

Liever /ˈliːvər/ *adv.* - Rather. From OE *lēofre*, cognate with German *lieber* (same meaning).

Lift /lɪft/ *n.* - The sky. From OE *lyft* ('air; the sky'), cognate with German *Luft* ('air').

Limmer /ˈlɪmər/ *n.* - A loose woman. Used as an insult. Etymology unclear; the author suggests some connection to French *limier* ('bloodhound'), but I am not convinced.

Lite /ləɪt, lɛɪt, leɪt/ *v.* - To rely on, to find. The author gives no etymology. I initially suspected this may be the same word as *lait* ('to seek'), but I now suspect it is from OE *wlītan*, 'to look; behold.' OE initial *wl-* clusters reduced to /l/ by, or during, the Middle English period.

Lithe /ləɪð, lɛɪð, leɪð/ *v.* - To listen. Of uncertain etymology, but there are parallels in meaning with ON *hljóð* ('hearing'), from the PGmc **hleuþą* ('hearing, listening'). It could be that an unattested OE root has given rise to the Cumbrian word, as the ON word does not have the correct reflex.

Lither /ˈlɪðər, ˈlɪdər/ *v.* - Lazy. Little etymology given, but clear parallels with ON *leiðr* ('uncomfortable, tired'). This is not the expected reflex, so it may be a dialectal borrowing from another northern dialect that came into contact with ON.

Luggs /lʊgz/ *n.* - Ears. Possibly from an unattested ON root, given similar cognates in modern Scandinavian languages. My father will sometimes jokingly threaten to give me a *clough round the lughole* (to strike somebody on the ear).

Lume /lɪəm/ *n.* - A tool. From OE *lōma* (same meaning). This is the expected development, and is cognate with English *loom* (the apparatus used for weaving). It also appears in its original OE sense in words like *heirloom*.

Luve /lɪəv/ *n.* - The palm of the hand. Author gives no etymology, but clearly a regular development from OE *lōf* (same meaning).

Marra /ˈmɛrə/ *n.* - A fellow. In later and modern usage, a workmate or friend. From ON *margr*, 'friendly.' Although it may not look it, this is a regular development. Northern OE generally dropped ON case endings when incorporating loan words from the language, so the *-r* was dropped, leaving *marg* (perhaps with the vowel adjusted to fit OE phonology). OE phonotactic rules meant that, in word-final /rg/ clusters, the /g/ was a fricative something like [ɣ] (a rasping, 'gutteral' sound made in the back of the throat). These [rɣ] clusters became *-row* in standard English, as in *barrow*, *arrow*. They did the same in Cumbrian, which turned *marg* into *marrow*.

However, as you may remember from earlier, Cumbrian massively reduces unstressed syllables, including the *-row* ending in words like *barrow* (which becomes /ˈbɛrə/) and *swallow* (/ˈswɛlə/). The same happened to *marrow*, producing /ˈmɛrə/. The fact that the author spells it *marra* here suggests this process was already complete, or at least productive, by 1677.

Meng /meŋ/ *v.* - To mix. From OE *mengan*, same meaning.

Mense /mens/ *n.* - Good manners. Author suggests OE *mennisc* ('mannish, manly'). I am not altogether convinced, although you could make a link in meaning between the two (perhaps something to do with proper men having good manners).

Mickell /ˈmɪkəl/ *det.* - Much. From unpalatalised OE *micel* or ON *mikill*: both would regularly give Cumbrian /ˈmɪkəl/.

Mould /ˈmɒld/ *n.* - A mole. This is parallelled by other forms such as *mowdywarp* (later, regular development with /l/ vocalised). Many forms are attested in Middle English, but no OE forms, so something like **moldeweorpe* is reconstructed.

Murk /mɔrk/ *adj.* - Dusky or dark. From OE unpalatalysed *myrce* (same meaning) or ON *myrkr* - both give the same later Cumbrian form.

Nate /nɛːt/ *v.* - To use. Must be connected to OE *notian* (same meaning) and German *nutzen*. Probably a loan from a dialect where the vowel was fronted before open-syllable lengthening took place.

Neb /neb/ *n.* - A nose or beak. From OE *nebb*, 'beak; face; nose.'

Nedder /'nedər/ *n.* - An adder, from OE *nœddre*. In standard English, this was subject to reanalysis, so that the phrase *a nadder* was re-interpreted as *an adder*. The word in standard English still lacks the original /n/.

Nowt /nɐʊt/ *n.* - Cattle. From ON *naut*, 'bull.' Related to OE *nēat* ('cattle'), but cannot be native; the OE word would give Cumbrian *neet* /niːt/. This is not to be confused with the unrelated but identically-pronounced word *nowt* ('nothing'), which comes from a different OE root.

Pace /pɛːs/ *n.* - Easter. From OE *pasce*.

Pick /pɪk/ *n.* - A pitch. From OE *pic*, unpalatalised form.

Read /riːd/ *v.* - To advise. From OE *rœdan*, same meaning. This is cognate with English 'read' as in 'to read a book,' but it better preserved the original meaning. Also cognate with German *reden* ('to speak').

Reek /riːk/ *n.* - Smoke. From OE *rēc*, unpalatalised form. I suspect this, or a similar northern form, is the origin of the standard English verb *reek* ('to smell unpleasant'). Cognate with German *Rauch*.

Ripe /rəɪp, rɐɪp, reɪp/ *v.* - To search into, investigate. Author gives OE *hrypan* ('to unsew'), but I cannot find this anywhere.

Sacless /'sɐkləs/ *adj.* - Guiltless, innocent. Interestingly, later dictionaries have it as 'spineless, pathetic.' From ON *saklaus*.

Same /sɛːm/ *n.* - Fat (the product). From OE *seim*.

Sark /sɐːrk/ *n.* - A shirt. From ON *serkr*.

Scarn /skɐːrn/ *n.* - Cow dung. Possibly from an Anglian variant of OE *scearn* ('dung') that lacks palatalisation, or more likely from ON *skarn*, survived by loan words in modern Scandinavian languages.

Scug /skʊg/ *n.* - Shade. From ON *skuggi*, 'shadow.'

Seggs /segz/ *n.* - Plants shaped like swords. From unpalatalised OE *secg*; its English cognate is 'sedge.'

Sib /sɪb/ *adj.* - Akin, similar. From OE *sibb*, same meaning, whence also English 'sibling.'

Sike /səɪk, sɐɪk, seɪk/ *n.* - A ditch. From unpalatalised OE *sīc*, 'waterway, ditch.'

Slott /slɒt/ *n.* - A door bolt. No attested OE root, but I suspect something like *slot-*, cognate with German *Schloß* ('door bolt; lock; castle').

Snell /snel/ *adj.* - Sharp, bitter. From OE *snel*, 'harsh; quick.' Cognate with German *schnell* ('quick').

Snite /snəɪt, snɐɪt, sneɪt/ *v.* - To blow. From OE *snȳtan,* 'to clear the nose.'

Snod /snɒd/ *adj.* - Smooth. Of uncertain origin.

Snude /snɪəd/ *n.* - A hair-dress. From OE *snōd*, same meaning.

Spelch /spelt͡ʃ/ *n.* - A bandage. From OE *spelc*, 'splinter.' This is a palatalised form presumably borrowed from a more southerly dialect, and a doublet of Cumbrian *spelk* ('splinter').

Stark /stɐːrk/ *adj.* - Stiff, strong. From OE *stearc,*'stiff, rigid.' Cognate with German *stark* ('strong').

Stegg /steg/ *n.* - A gander, male goose. From ON *steggr*.

Stiddy /ˈstɪdiː/ *n.* - An anvil. From ON *steði*, same meaning. This may be an early example of *i* and *e* being used interchangeably in writing because the two vowels had such similar qualities.

Stoond /stʊnd/ *n.* - Pain. From OE *stund*, 'exertion; pain.'

Strand /strɐnd/ *n.* - A shoreline. OE *strand*, same meaning.

Streak /striːk/ *v.* - To stretch. From unpalatalised OE *streccan*.

Swarth /swɐːrθ/ *n.* - A ghost. Further detail in the chapter on folklore. From OE *sweart,* 'black.'

Swelt /swelt/ *v.* - To faint, pass out. From OE *sweltan*, 'to die.'

Theek /θiːk/ *n.* - Thatch. From OE *þaca*, 'covering; roof; thatch.' Possibly an inter-dialectal borrowing.

This geats /ðɪs gɛəts, -gɪɛts/ - In this way; thus. Literally 'this road(s).' See *geat*.

Thole /θwɔːl/ *v.* - To suffer. From OE *þolian*, same meaning.

Threep /θriːp/ *v.* To urge. From OE *þrēapian*, 'to reprehend.'

Tume /tɪəm/ *adj.* - Empty. From OE *tōm*, same meaning.

Twinter /ˈtwɪntər/ *n.* - A sheep two winters old; equivalent to *twee + winter.*

Weat /wɛət, wiɐt/ *v.* - To know. From OE *wāt* (1st person sing.) same meaning. Cognate with German *weiß*, ditto.

Weell /wiːl/ *v.* - To choose. Probably from an unattested OE root. Cognate with German *wählen* (same meaning).

Wheem /ʍiːm/ *adj.* - Calm. From OE *gecwēme*, 'pleasant.' Remember that *cw-* clusters become voiceless *w* in Cumbrian.

Wheen-cat /ʍiːn kɐt/ *n.* - A she-cat. From OE *cwēn* ('woman') + *catt* ('cat'). The *wheen* is cognate with English *Queen*.

Whilk /ʍɪlk/ *det.* - Which. From OE *hwylc*, same meaning.

Yett /jet/ *n.* - Gate. Presumably a north-eastern Cumbrian form; the north-western form would be *yat*. This shows descent from the original OE form *geat*, which had initial /j/, rather than the ON form that gives standard English *gate* (with initial /g/).

Yud /jʊd/ *v.* - Went. Past simple of *gan, gang* ('to go'). Expected reflex from OE *ēode* ('went'), which was commonly used in all dialects of OE but disappeared early on in the south.

General Glossary

Aback on, *prep.* - Behind.
Abuun, *prep.* - Above
Ahint, *prep.* - Behind.
Anent, *prep.* - On top of.
Bam, *n.* - A trick.
Beest, *n.* - A cow.
Beetle, *v.* - To wash clothes in a river by suspending them on a wet rock and hitting them with a mallet.
Bray, *v.* - To hit, strike.
Brekkin in, *n.* - A breaking-in; to wear clothes to make them less stiff and more comfortable.
Brock, *n.* - A badger.
Car, *n.* - A cart.
Carlin sark, *n.* - A working-shirt.
Cokert, gokert, *n.* - Awkward, inarticulate.
Corse, *n.* - A corpse.
Cu, *n.* - A cow.
Deid, *adj.* - Dead.
Deu, *v.* - To do.
Ee, *n.* - An eye.
Et, - (Verb infinitive marker).
Fain, *adj.* - Glad, happy.
Farder, *adv.* - Farther.
Fo, *v.* - Fall.
Frow, *n.* - An austere woman.
Fud, *n.* - Food.
Fwok, fwoke, fwoak, *n.* - People.
Fworganger, *n.* - Ancestor.

Fworset, *v.* - To forset, ambush.
Ga, *v.* - To go.
Gan, *v.* To go.
Gang, *v.* - To go.
Gedder, *v.* - To gather.
Gif, *conj.* - If.
Girse, *n.* - Grass.
Girt, *adj.* - Great, big.
Grean, *n.* - Groan.
Gud, *adj.* - Good.
Heamm, yam, *n.* - Home.
Hest, *n.* - Horse.
Hoaf, *n.* -Half.
Ho'penny, *n.* - Ha'penny.
Hus, *n.* - House.
I soat - (Of an animal) dead; literally 'in salt' (i.e. preserving).
Iv, *prep.* - On; for other applications, see section of syntax.
Iv late - Recently.
Kersemas, *n.* - Christmas.
Koaf, *n.* - Calf.
Kye, *n.* - Cattle.
Lee, *n.* - Lie; falsehood.
Leuk, *v.* - To look.
Leuv, *n.* - Love.
Lig, *v.* - Lie.
Lowp, *v.* - Jump, leap.
Mair, *det.* - More.
Maister, *n.* - Master.
Med, *n.* - Might.
Meear, *n.* - Mare; female horse.
Mowdywarp, *n.* - Mole.

Mus, *n.* - Mouse.
Nar on, *adv.* - Near to; almost.
Neest, *adj.* - Next.
Neet, *n.* - Night.
Neuk, niuk, *n.* - Nook; corner; dwelling, hovel.
Nin, *pron.* - None; not.
Nobut, *adv.* - Only.
Nowder, *det.* - Neither.
Od skerse - Minced oath for 'God's curse.'
Od's wuns an' deeth - Minced oath for 'God's wounds and death.'
Owwer, *prep.* - Over.
Pack-lead, *n.* - A load to put on the back of a horse.
Plet, *v.* - To plait.
Queer, *adj.* - Strange; ill.
Rebm, *n.* - Raven.
Reet, *adj.* - Right.
Sall, *v.* - Shall, will.
Sattle, *n.* - Seat.
Sek, *det.* - Such.
Sek as, sek leyke, *prep.* - Such as; similarly to.

Setterda, *n.* - Saturday.
Seun, *adv.* - Soon; early.
Shun, *n.* - Shoes.
Skiul, *n.* - School.
Slattery, *adj.* - (Of weather) rainy.
Snapin, *n.* - A shunning; an act designed to get somebody out of the way.
Soat, *n.* - Salt.
Stean, *n.* - Stone.
Taties, *n.* - Potatoes.
Til, *prep.* - To (when not an infinitive marker).
Torfor, *v.* - To perish; to die.
Waddent, *v.* - Would not.
Ware brass, *v.* - To spend money, especially wastefully.
Whyte, *adv.* - Quite.
Wo, *n.* - A wall.
Wohl, *n.* - A hole.
Woo, *n.* - Wool.
Yal, *n.* - Beer, ale.
Yan, *num.* - One.
Yance, yence, *adv.* - Once.
Yet, yit, *adv.* - Yet; still.

List of Images

Front cover. A photograph of my great-grandparents making hay, presumably in the 1930s or 1940s.

29. A Swaledale sheep with long wool, characteristic of periods where wool was in high demand.

42. A sketch of the pitch contours of an excerpt of speech from the previous chapter, showing intonation.

49. The red grouse, *Lagopus lagopus scotia*. Found and hunted in the moors of western Cumbria.

66. A ceramic owl whistle made by my grandmother, after another potter whose name I do not know. She worked out how to make the whistle by close examination of an original, and needed no instruction. She was an exceptional potter and an exceptional person beyond anybody else I know. I may put some memories of her into words one day, but I did not feel that it was appropriate to do so here.

74. Shepherds crooks. There is a long tradition in Cumbria of stylised shepherds crooks. These are produced by makers and sold to this day at agricultural shows.

94. Two sheep in profile. The top one is a Herdwick; the bottom one is somewhere between a Rough Fell and a Swaledale.

104. A woman's clothing in the 19th century, including a checked camperdown *brat* ('apron').

116. A man's clothing in the 19th century. I did not give the man a face and omit to give the woman one for mysoginistic reasons; in drawing them, the woman's face turned out much worse. I tried to get rid of the man's face digitally, but it looked awful, so on balance I have kept it.

147. A wooden-soled clog, the common working footwear of much of northern England until the 20th century.

164. A carving from the Gosforth Cross of a scene from Norse mythology, showing Þórr and Hýmir fishing in the great sea that surrounds the world. There are fish in the original carving which I have not included. Of course, it could just be two men fishing, but its proximity to other carvings more explicitly resembling Norse mythological scenes, and its presence on a cross bearing Scandinavian motifs, has led scholars to the conclusion that it is meant to be Þórr and Hýmir.

Sources & Further Reading

Brilioth, B. 1913. *A Grammar of the Dialect of Lorton (Cumberland) Historical & Descriptive.*

Orton, H. 1962. *Survey of English Dialects: the Six Northern Counties and the Isle of Man.*

The British Library's recordings from the Survey of English Dialects, available online at the time of writing.

Ferguson, R. 1873. *The Dialect of Cumberland.*

Anderson, R. 1870[49]. *Ballads in the Cumberland Dialect.*

Dickinson, W. 1878. *A Glossary of Words and Phrases Pertaining to the Dialect of Cumberland.*

Prevost, E. & Dickson Brown, S. 1905. *A Supplement to the Glossary of the Dialect of Cumberland.*

Sparke, A. 1907. *A Bibliography of the Dialect Literature of Cumberland & Westmorland.*

Gibson, A. 1891. *The Folk Speech of Cumberland & Some Districts Adjacent.*

Henderson, W. 1879. *Notes on the Folklore of the Northern Counties of England & the Borders.*

Wheeler, A. 1790. *The Westmorland Dialect, in Three Familiar Dialogues.*

Relph, J. 1743. *A Miscellany of Poems.*

Stenroos, M; Mäkinen, M; Horobin, S; Smith, J. 2011. The Middle English Grammar Corpus, version 2011.1. University of Stavanger.

Rebanks, J. 2015. *The Shepherd's Life.*

McCormick, T. 2018. *Lake District Fell Farming: Historical & Literary Perspectives.*

Hall, I. 2017. *Thorneythwaite Farm, Borrowdale.*

Hickey, R. (ed.) 2015. *Researching Northern English.*

Smith, J. 2007. *Sound Change & the History of English.*

Walcott, M. 1870. *Glossary of Words in the Cumbrian Dialect.* In Transactions of the Royal Society of Literature of the United Kingdom, Second Series, Vol. 4.

---

[49] The archive edition I found was dated 1870, but many of the ballads were dated 1802.

Acknowledgements

Thank you to dad, Hazel, and the rest of my family, particularly those on my father's side who have inspired and informed aspects of this book.

Many, many thanks also to my school English teachers, in particular Roger Taylor, Emily Short and Gemma May.

Finally, thank you to Börje Brilioth, and other researchers who have taken the time to document the dialect in its various past iterations.

Printed in Great Britain
by Amazon